REBOOTING
ASSESSMENT

A Practical Guide for Balancing Conversations, Performances, and Products

DAMIAN COOPER
With Jeff Catania

Solution Tree | Press

a division of
Solution Tree

555 North Morton Street
Bloomington, IN 47404
800.733.6786 (toll free) / 812.336.7700
FAX: 812.336.7790

email: info@SolutionTree.com
SolutionTree.com

Visit **go.SolutionTree.com/assessment** to download the free reproducibles in this book.

Printed in the United States of America

Library of Congress Cataloging-in-Publication Data

Names: Cooper, Damian, author.
Title: Rebooting assessment : a practical guide for balancing
   conversations, performances, and products / Damian Cooper.
Description: Bloomington, IN : Solution Tree Press, 2021. | Includes
   bibliographical references and index.
Identifiers: LCCN 2021038533 (print) | LCCN 2021038534 (ebook) | ISBN
   9781952812316 (paperback) | ISBN 9781952812323 (ebook)
Subjects: LCSH: Educational tests and measurements--Technological
   innovations. | Students--Rating of--Technological innovations.
Classification: LCC LB3060.5 .C67 2021 (print) | LCC LB3060.5 (ebook) |
   DDC 371.26--dc23
LC record available at https://lccn.loc.gov/2021038533
LC ebook record available at https://lccn.loc.gov/2021038534

Solution Tree
Jeffrey C. Jones, CEO
Edmund M. Ackerman, President

Solution Tree Press
President and Publisher: Douglas M. Rife
Associate Publisher: Sarah Payne-Mills
Art Director: Rian Anderson
Managing Production Editor: Kendra Slayton
Editorial Director: Todd Brakke
Copy Chief: Jessi Finn
Content Development Specialist: Amy Rubenstein
Copy Editor: Evie Madsen
Proofreader: Elisabeth Abrams
Text and Cover Designer: Rian Anderson
Editorial Assistants: Sarah Ludwig and Elijah Oates

For our dear friend and trusted
colleague, David Steele

Acknowledgments

Rebooting Assessment began as an online professional development course for *validating observation and conversation when assessing learning* (VOCAL). My dear friends and colleagues, David Steele and Jeff Catania, were equal partners in the creation and publishing of that course and the refinement of our VOCAL approach to balanced assessment. Jeff also worked with me throughout the development of this book, writing chapter 4 in its entirety, mentoring me in all matters involving technology, and providing invaluable ideas, suggestions, and support.

Because the video clips (linked through QR codes) throughout this book and much of *Rebooting Assessment*'s written content derive from our VOCAL online course, I wish to say a huge "thank you!" to the following wonderful, trailblazing educators who were involved in that project along with the schools they worked in at that time.

- From Dr. Frank J. Hayden Secondary School in Burlington, Ontario: Stephanie Girvan, secondary mathematics teacher; Jamie Mitchell, mathematics teacher and mathematics program leader; Todd Malarczuk, secondary mathematics teacher; and Jacqueline Newton, principal

- From Forest Trail Public School in Oakville, Ontario: Holly Moniz, intermediate teacher, and Steve Pilibbossian, principal

- From Oodenawi Public School in Oakville, Ontario: Jacqueline (Jackie) Clarke, third-grade teacher, and Gail McDonald, principal

- From Iroquois Ridge High School in Oakville, Ontario: Helen Hills, secondary English teacher, and Darlene White, principal

- From the team at *Enable Education* (https://enableeducation.com) for launching the VOCAL online course: Ben Zimmer, Dave Zimmer, Matt Paterson, Ruth Riddle, and Octavian Ciubotariu

For their support in the writing of this book, I'd also like to thank Dylan Wiliam and Emma Steele. Dylan, thank you for your inspiration and for contributing invaluable suggestions to the draft manuscript. Emma Steele created the original design for *Rebooting Assessment*. Huge thanks, Emma.

I would like to thank everyone at Solution Tree for their support and professionalism as we collaborated on this project, especially Douglas Rife, Todd Brakke, Kendra Slayton, Amy Rubenstein, Sarah Payne-Mills, and Rian Anderson. I would also like to extend my sincere appreciation to the reviewers of the draft manuscript for their insightful comments and welcome suggestions.

My partner, Nanci Wakeman, has been supportive and patient, and she provided numerous suggestions, insights, and sound advice throughout this project. Thank you, Nanci.

To all my dear colleagues and friends in the Canadian Assessment for Learning Network (CAfLN; https://cafln.ca): you continue to amaze and inspire me with your passion for assessment and learning. A special acknowledgment goes to my fellow founding members of CAfLN, Lorna Earl and Ken O'Connor.

Finally, I must acknowledge my debt to the late Grant Wiggins, whose wisdom and vision have influenced all my professional work since 1994. Grant, may your memory live on in our schools.

—Damian Cooper, Clarkson, Ontario, February 2021

TABLE OF CONTENTS

Reproducible pages are in italics.

Chapter 04

How Can I Use Technology to Support Assessment? 74

Chapter 05

How Do I Use the VOCAL Approach to Improve Learning? 104

Chapter 06

How Should I Communicate About Learning in the Digital Age? 126

Epilogue

Appendix

About the Authors

Damian Cooper is an independent educational consultant who specializes in helping schools and school districts across North America and internationally improve their instructional and assessment skills. In his varied career, Damian has been a secondary English language arts, special education, and drama teacher; a department head; a librarian; and a school consultant. He has specialized in student assessment for more than thirty years. Damian served as assessment consultant to the School Division of Nelson Education. Prior to that, he was coordinator of assessment and evaluation for the Halton District School Board in Burlington, Ontario. Damian is a cofounder and past president of the Canadian Assessment for Learning Network (CAfLN).

Damian's international reputation rests on his wide-ranging experience as an educator, his deep understanding of assessment, and his no-nonsense, common-sense approach to what works in schools.

Damian's previous publications, *Talk About Assessment: Strategies and Tools to Improve Learning*; *Talk About Assessment: High School Strategies and Tools*; and *Redefining Fair: How to Plan, Assess, and Grade for Excellence in Mixed-Ability Classrooms*, are bestsellers.

Visit *Plan, Teach, Assess* (www.planteachassess.com) or follow @cooperd1954 on Twitter to learn more about Damian's work.

Jeff Catania led a variety of K–12 program areas for the Halton District School Board in Burlington, Ontario, including applied learning, assessment and evaluation, information technology in the classroom, mathematics, and restorative practices. He conceived and launched Halton's ongoing bring your own device (BYOD), cloud computing, eLearning, and mindfulness programs for staff and students.

Jeff has facilitated hundreds of staff learning experiences across North America and is a contributing author to

Talk About Assessment: High School Strategies and Tools (with Damian Cooper) and *The Joy of X: Mathematics Teaching in Grades 7–12* (with Shirley Dalrymple and George Gadanidis).

Jeff now enjoys farm life, provides mathematics therapy, facilitates a support group for betrayed partners, and leads adult learning experiences to explore and deepen peace, joy, flow, and love.

Visit https://alove.ca to learn more about Jeff's work.

To book Damian Cooper or Jeff Catania for professional development, contact pd@SolutionTree.com.

Introduction

I've been an educator since 1979, and throughout most of that time, I have been on a personal crusade to instill balance and sanity to educational assessment. From my youth as a student at the Salesian College in Farnborough, England, I've had a sense that something was seriously amiss in the way the education system deemed my peers and I suitable (or not) for a university education (see figure I.1). Achieve an overall passing grade on the state-mandated 11+ Examination, and you received a scholarship (government-funded tuition at grammar school), the required route to university. My older brother, Vince, knew from his early teens that he wanted to become a doctor. But he almost didn't make it into University of Bristol to study science because he had trouble memorizing the thousands of facts necessary to get high grades on three A-level General Certificate of Education examinations. Years later, Vince traveled to McMaster University in Hamilton, Ontario, to learn firsthand about the hands-on, practical examinations its faculty of medicine uses (rather than rote memorization) to certify young doctors. Someone had finally seen the light!

**Figure I.1:
It's time to question the primacy of written examinations.**

> "
>
> *The written exam is in danger of becoming an anachronism in this age of digital natives who could more easily throw together a multimedia presentation than they could handwrite a persuasive essay. We should perhaps question which of those options is most important in modern society—or if both, in what balance—and design assessment that reflects this.*
>
> *The pervasiveness of the internet means that in the developed world at least we have information at our fingertips at any time. It is therefore no longer necessary to memorise lots and lots of facts but more important to be able to judge the reliability and accuracy of the information we find online.*
>
> *This raises the question of whether it might even be desirable in examinations of the future to allow students access to the internet, testing not what they know so much as their ability to learn something new quickly and accurately.*
> *(RM Results, n.d., p. 24)*

Gradually, I came to the realization that the privileged status that secure, timed, written tests and examinations enjoyed in the context of educational assessment and evaluation was problematic, given that the demonstration of skills and the ability to express one's opinions and beliefs orally were equally valid indicators of proficiency. And I came to this realization decades before the internet placed factual knowledge at everyone's fingertips!

Fast forward to 1979 and my career as a high school English teacher. Initially, I fell in line with my colleagues whose assessment practices looked exactly the same as those my former teachers employed—assign innumerable essays, along with the occasional book report and piece of creative writing; collect the polished drafts of these; correct *all* the errors myself; and return the marked work with the naive and absurd belief that students would improve their subsequent efforts (see figure I.2).

To be fair, those students who were already excelling did improve marginally, their desire for honors status for their year-end grades solely motivating them. My assessment methods simply maintained the status quo for the vast majority of my students. However, my school leaders believed I was doing my job, given each principal I worked for operated according to norm-referenced beliefs— evaluating each student in relation to his or her peers, rather than against known public standards (criterion-referenced)—and monitoring teachers' grade distributions by examining class medians.

Things changed when I moved to a school serving a population consisting mostly of students at risk. The practices I had come to rely on failed miserably. Most students didn't do the work I assigned, and those who attempted the work submitted products that were either illegible, incoherent, or both. So I made the following three major changes to my assessment routine (Cooper, 2011).

1. I changed *homework* to *classwork*, meaning students completed most writing under my direct supervision.

2. I implemented a clear writing process regimen that included having students develop an initial idea, jotting down rough notes, creating a rough first draft, revising and editing this draft, and finally submitting a polished draft.

Figure I.2:
Traditional marking rarely results in deep student learning because the teacher is doing the thinking.

3. I shifted the focus of assessment from summative to formative, the latter differentiated to each student based on the gaps I identified in each student's skills.

The impact of these changes was rapid and significant: students' confidence in their potential to improve increased; knowing the specific skills they needed to focus on while knowing where to channel their energy enabled them to shift from a fixed to a growth mindset (Dweck, 2016).

Fast forward once more to my time as a consultant, initially with a large Canadian school district in 1990 and then independently, beginning in 2005. Over time, I became increasingly passionate about the power of assessment to improve learning. I have promoted balanced, triangulated assessment practices that include observing what learners do through performances and listening to them reveal their understanding through conversations.

Yet, despite my efforts and those of my colleagues, classroom assessment hasn't changed much during my forty-plus years as an educator. Albert Einstein purportedly defined *insanity* as doing the same thing over and over again and expecting different results (as cited in Wilczek, 2015). Certainly, beyond the primary grades (K–2), assessment remains preoccupied with testing, and that testing focuses largely on the extent to which students can memorize large amounts of information. This memorization-driven assessment model historically evolved at a time when education involved learned people—often the clergy—imparting factual knowledge to unlearned pupils. Since written texts and, later, printed texts were in short supply, becoming educated meant committing to memory the body of knowledge contained in those rare texts. Fast forward to the information age and now the digital age, and knowledge is now a mere click away, for everyone.

So why hasn't more of the educational community awakened to the realization that assessment needs to change dramatically? After working for more than thirty years in a variety of consulting roles, I have concluded that the primary reasons for this intractability include a pervasive conservatism within the educational community, an unwillingness on the part of senior management to hold teachers accountable for change, a research-averse culture, and a serious lack of system-wide, mandatory professional development in favor of voluntary, ad hoc approaches to ongoing teacher improvement.

It is this disconnect that has led me to write *Rebooting Assessment*. It is my attempt to nudge student assessment into the modern era through a technology-supported and balanced approach that includes conversations and performances as key components in a teacher's toolkit (see figure I.3). In the rest of this introduction, I detail some of the ways assessment needs to change; how balanced and triangulated assessment leads to deeper student engagement, greater equity, and increased reliability; and how to engage with *Rebooting Assessment*.

Figure I.3:
Nudging
assessment into
the digital age.

Source: © 2017 by Plan Teach Assess. Used with permission.

How Assessment Needs to Change

Given the problems with traditional forms of assessment, it's fair to ask, "What does it mean to reboot assessment for today's schools?" From my perspective, there are four fundamental changes that must occur.

1. Assessment needs to be balanced, including evidence teachers gather through conversations with students and performance-based observations that reveal students' learning, as well as the typical assessment of student-constructed products.

2. The focus of assessment needs to shift from *summative* to *formative*. The primary purpose of assessment must be to improve learning as it occurs as part of a prescriptive approach, not to measure it after the fact as a learning autopsy.

3. Students must become essential players in their own assessment. The *metacognitive function of assessment*, in which students self-assess and reflect on their own thinking and learning, must receive at least as much attention as teacher-directed components.

4. Communication to parents or guardians and the larger community about student learning must shift from a reliance on numerical grades to standards-based descriptions of understanding and competency, along with samples of evidence (recorded conversations and performances and physical products).

Throughout this book, Jeff Catania (my valued partner in this work) and I explore each of these imperatives.

In the twentieth century, the standardised test approach could be valid and reliable, though never perfect. However, in the twenty-first century landscape, where the demands go beyond just knowledge and technical skills, there is, indeed, a need for an "assessment renaissance" so that the desired attributes can be meaningfully monitored or measured. (Hill & Barber, 2014, p. 1)

Balanced and Triangulated Assessment

When we recommend that teachers incorporate assessment through conversations and performance-based observations, many raise concerns such as, "It's too subjective and unreliable," "Parents want to see grades," and "How do I keep track of what I see and hear students doing?" Such resistance doesn't factor in the role of technology to support these efforts, particularly the prevalence of smartphones and tablets. These easy-to-use mobile technologies are fully capable of capturing conversational and performance-based evidence of student learning in real time.

Rebooting Assessment shows teachers how balancing their *assessment portfolio* (the assessments they employ and their approach to reporting on assessed learning) with video and other forms of digital evidence not only improves assessment reliability but also increases equity of opportunity for students who struggle with paper-based assessments and other product-based formats. This resource takes teachers right into classrooms where their peers are experimenting with the many ways handheld devices

> **"** *Traditional assessment practices were not designed to test the higher order thinking and learning skills. They are skills that may be better assessed through observational assessment, perhaps over time, rather than through a paper and pen exercise that—while excellent at allowing students to show knowledge of theory—is limited in allowing students to demonstrate application and offers only a "snapshot in time." (RM Results, n.d., p. 8)*

can capture, in the moment, how students show what they know, understand, and are able to do.

While we see mobile devices in increasing numbers of classrooms, few teachers seem to realize their potential for assessment. For example, a primary teacher uses a tablet to record students reading aloud but then relies on a standardized test to derive a score for their individual reading skills. A science teacher encourages students to use their smartphones in class to search for fascinating facts related to a lesson but then relies exclusively on written lab reports and tests to assess student learning. And so it's time for some nudging.

In this resource, teachers will find numerous QR codes linked to online videos that will help them unlock the amazing power of technology to connect assessment with instruction. These videos demonstrate how to capture a few seconds of each student *speaking* or *doing* and then how to use this evidence to decide on instructional entry points; provide students with feedback and other supports; or speak to parents or guardians about their child's progress.

All the videos are captured using smartphones and tablets (figure I.4). So, Jeff and I are practicing what we preach by employing the very same tools and strategies those videos feature. Commentary that highlights the strategies they

Figure I.4:
Capturing a student performance on a smartphone.

Source: © 2017 by Plan Teach Assess. Used with permission.

depict, as well as professional learning activities that promote application, collaboration, and reflection, accompany the videos.

Our goal is for you to see for yourself the powerful, positive impact a balanced approach to assessment (that includes conversations and performances) can have on teaching and learning in your classroom and how mobile technologies make assessing in this way practical and effective for all teachers and students.

Understandably, a change of this magnitude causes anxiety. Here's a sample of the questions we hear most frequently from teachers when we advocate this approach.

- "What are the benefits of conversations and performances?"
- "Isn't assessing conversations and performances more subjective than assessing a written or physical product?"
- "What does conversation- and performance-based evidence look like in subjects like mathematics and science?"
- "How do I involve students in these kinds of assessments?"
- "How do I find the time to talk to and observe all my students?"
- "How do I convince parents or guardians to accept assessment based on conversations and performances?"
- "How many conversations and performances do I need to facilitate for each student?"

While we address all these questions in due course, let me address the second. We need to remind ourselves that measurement error occurs every time teachers assess student learning. Teachers can never have 100 percent confidence in the conclusions they reach about learning. Former educator and prolific author Ruth Sutton (1991) put it best:

> It is worth noting, right from the start, that assessment is a human process, conducted by and with human beings, and subject inevitably to the frailties of human judgement. However crisp and objective we might try to make it, and however neatly quantifiable may be our results, assessment is closer to an art than a science. It is, after all, an exercise in human communication. (p. 2)

Sutton (1991) is talking about *reliability*, which is a measure of the confidence teachers have in the data they gather. As noted previously, no assessment is 100 percent accurate. But reliability is not always of critical importance. The purpose of formative assessment—which includes assessment *for* learning and assessment *as* learning—is to improve learning, *not* measure it (see figure I.5, page 8). For the purposes of this text, think of each of these approaches to formative assessment as follows.

- **Assessment *for* learning:** This aspect of formative assessment emphasizes that teachers use assessment data to drive instruction, or as chapter 1 (page 12) notes, to inform learning during the instructional process (Stiggins, 2005; Wiliam, 2018).
- **Assessment *as* learning:** This aspect of formative assessment puts the onus on students to self-monitor their learning and use the data to achieve specific learning goals (Earl, 2013).

Figure I.5: The purpose of formative assessment is to improve learning, *not* measure it.

> There has been a shift worldwide from seeing assessment as a "judgement" of what students have learned to a tool to further understanding what students are learning, feeding back into their ongoing development. It is of little benefit to have students leaving education with gaps in their knowledge—least of all the student—hence, formative assessment has been growing in importance in many parts of the world, complementing the often still all-important summative assessments. (RM Results, n.d., p. 6)

For formative assessment to be truly effective, it must be responsive to the differing needs of students. But as soon as teachers begin differentiating formative assessment to further the learning of students who have differing needs, they seriously compromise reliability—and that's just fine! Reliability, a measure of confidence based on consistency, is not important when a teacher is using individualized formative assessment that responds to each student's specific learning needs.

There are times, however, when reliability is of great importance. For example, when an assessment's purpose is *summative*—such as end-of-unit, end-of-term, and end-of-course assessments—teachers should be seriously concerned with reliability. Why? Because teachers must have confidence in the judgments they make about whether students are proficient with respect to essential knowledge, understanding, and skills. We explore this balance more deeply in chapter 1 (page 12).

Pause and Reflect

Reflect on and discuss the following comments with a colleague.

- Assessment is subject to the frailties of human judgment.
  - Reliability may well go out the window when assessment is formative.
  - Reliability is critical when assessment is summative.

How to Engage With *Rebooting Assessment*

In the technology world, *rebooting* a computer or handheld device is something people do when the hardware or software stops working the way it's supposed to. The thinking is, whatever the problem is, a reboot will clear it out so the device can perform—and it frequently works! In this resource, we think of assessment in the same way. *Assessment* is a valuable and essential tool for teachers to measure learning and determine necessary course corrections for instruction based on data about what students know, understand, and can do. But educators frequently don't *use* assessment in ways that enable these goals. Furthermore, an internet-connected world filled with readily available and portable technology expands teachers' assessment options. Given these factors, we think assessment is overdue for a reboot of its own, and this resource will help you do just that.

Note, first, we do *not* recommend that you sit down and read this book cover to cover. Why? Because *Rebooting Assessment* began as the VOCAL online course that Jeff Catania, David Steele, and I developed for teachers. (Visit www.wavelearningsolutions .com/vocal to learn more about this course.) The course instructs educators in what we call the *VOCAL approach*, which we've adapted and applied to this resource as an avenue for teachers to establish and sustain balanced assessment practices that utilize student conversations and performances along with products. As the graphic in figure I.6 illustrates, VOCAL advocates that teachers—*in addition to* relying on traditional assessment methods around physical products—observe and listen to students showing evidence of their acquisition of curriculum content and skills as they reveal their understanding through conversations and performances. By using digital devices like smartphones and tablets to record these interactions, teachers and students can capture evidence of learning in the moment, both to further learning and to share learning with stakeholders ranging from parents or guardians to school administrators. (For simplicity going forward, note our use of the descriptor *parent* includes adults acting as a student's legal guardian.)

Source: © 2017 by Plan Teach Assess. Used with permission.

Figure I.6: The VOCAL approach.

We designed the VOCAL approach to enable small groups of teachers to use digital devices at their own pace to learn and then apply their learning to classroom assessment according to their respective comfort levels. We suggest you engage with *Rebooting Assessment* in the same way: read, view, reflect, discuss, try, revise, read more.

Why read and view? This resource connects to numerous video clips, immediately accessible by scanning the QR codes, that feature teachers and students engaged in balanced assessment tasks. Seeing teachers implementing the strategies and processes this book describes will enable you to gain a much deeper understanding than text would allow.

The video clips are essential to *Rebooting Assessment* because they take you directly into classrooms to see teachers implementing the VOCAL approach. Watch as many of the videos as you wish. We excerpt key messaging and moments so you can review key comments the featured teachers and students make. We strongly encourage you to discuss both the VOCAL concepts and the video content with your colleagues, either in person or online, to deepen your understanding (see figure I.7).

Figure I.7: Collaboration with colleagues will enhance your VOCAL approach.

We realize that broadening your assessment practice to include conversations and performance-based observations may represent a significant departure from your current practice, so we've differentiated *Rebooting Assessment* to reflect differing personal comfort levels with using technology to support a VOCAL approach. Key to this differentiation is the *Teacher-Readiness Scale* we introduce in chapter 1 (page 27), which enables you to find your own comfort level with the ideas and approaches this book presents.

We organized *Rebooting Assessment* into six chapters. Depending on your current familiarity with assessing through conversations and performances and using technology to capture and share evidence of student learning, you may or may not choose to read them chronologically. Each chapter answers a vital question related to the VOCAL approach. Chapter 1 introduces the concept of balanced assessment and why it's important. Chapter 2 explains how teachers can plan their instruction and curriculum around balanced assessment. Chapter 3 clarifies how to assess through conversations and performance-based observations. Chapter 4 answers questions about the varying extents to which teachers can use technology to support a VOCAL approach. Chapter 5 illustrates how teachers can use five components of assessment *for* learning in conjunction with a VOCAL approach to improve learning outcomes. Finally, chapter 6 answers questions about how teachers can best communicate information about learning and assessment in the digital age.

There are numerous features common to all chapters. As noted, we include links to supporting videos in the form of QR codes throughout the book. To view them, scan the QR code with your smartphone or tablet. *Pause and Reflect* boxes are an opportunity to do just that—individually or with your colleagues. *It's About Time* boxes anticipate and address challenges involving time management you are likely to identify with or encounter as you implement the changes we propose. There are numerous *Shift and Share* figures throughout the book that serve as an invitation to apply what you've been learning in a given chapter to your own classroom context. This is a differentiated element, offering a choice of tasks that align with chapter 1's Teacher-Readiness Scale. We urge you to seek out one or more colleagues with whom to discuss your learning and to collaboratively plan how you will apply that learning. Finally, each chapter closes first with a *Questions About . . .* section that addresses specific frequently asked questions about the chapter topic, and then a simple and concise *Key Messages* summary from each chapter.

A concluding appendix offers reference lists for all the video URLs in this book as well as the Shift and Share figures. It also includes a collection of the classroom tools featured in the text and videos throughout this book. Visit **go.SolutionTree.com/assessment** to access digital, reproducible versions of these online tools.

And now it's time to dive in (see figure I.8)!

Figure I.8: The best way to learn about balanced assessment is to take the plunge.

Why Is Balanced Assessment Important?

Simply put, *balanced assessment* means recognizing that complex educational outcomes, such as critical thinking, creativity, communication, and collaboration, demand a varied and flexible approach to assessment. That flexibility requires an appropriate—though not necessarily equal—balance of conversations, performances, and products, described as follows.

- **Conversations:** As distinct from oral presentations, conversations between students and between students and teachers provide direct insight into students' thinking and depth of understanding. Because conversation is unrehearsed and free-flowing, it provides evidence of critical thinking as students process, analyze, evaluate, and respond to differing points of view, possible approaches and solutions, differing opinions, and competing points of view. The assessor's role is to prompt, listen, respond, and possibly record the conversation.

- **Performances:** These include any and all activities in which students actively demonstrate one or more competencies. A performance may be as simple as reading a text passage aloud or as complex as a multiday, authentic simulation in which students adopt roles and respond to real-world problems such as climate change, a pandemic, or a famine. The assessor, whether teacher, peer, or external expert, relies on observation as students demonstrate targeted competencies.

- **Products:** These include any and all student-generated work. Products, often called artifacts, may include written work, models, artwork, dioramas, and so on. The assessor typically collects and marks products.

Balancing assessment may sound simple enough, initially. But education's longstanding default to written assessment has caused many grades 3–12 teachers to be most comfortable assigning, collecting, and marking products and far less willing to consider using conversations and performances as legitimate and rigorous ways to assess student learning.

However, students are growing up in a world where memorizing lots of things is far less important than being able to *do* a lot of things (Partnership for 21st Century Learning, 2019). That's a very simple way of saying that in a world where information

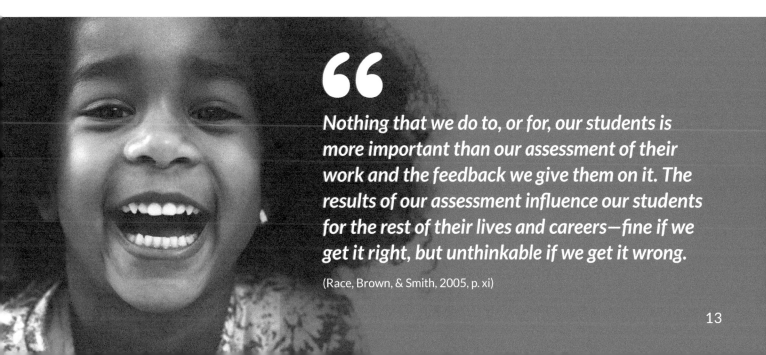

66

Nothing that we do to, or for, our students is more important than our assessment of their work and the feedback we give them on it. The results of our assessment influence our students for the rest of their lives and careers—fine if we get it right, but unthinkable if we get it wrong.

(Race, Brown, & Smith, 2005, p. xi)

about anything and everything is a click or tap away, competence has become more important than encyclopedic knowledge.

Teachers who understand balanced assessment ensure they devote appropriate time and energy to observing student performances and engaging them in conversation as they demonstrate skills, in addition to collecting physical artifacts or products that reflect their learning. These teachers understand that the assessment approach they select at any given moment—a performance task, an oral or conversational task, or a product—must match the type of learning outcomes they teach. Just as the driving examiner requires a combination of a written test to assess the rules of the road, an in-car road test to assess skills, and oral questioning to assess understanding and attitude to certify a driver as proficient, effective teachers understand they must employ a variety of assessment modes for the same purpose—to determine student proficiency (see figure 1.1). *Assessment mode* refers to the type of strategy a teacher selects to have students demonstrate learning: oral communication, performance task, or student product. The assessor,

whether teacher or peer, correspondingly listens to, observes, or marks the work to provide feedback (formative) or a score (summative). Note that scoring should be the exclusive responsibility of the teacher.

To help you understand the impact of balanced assessment, this chapter highlights how the VOCAL approach to assessment supports achieving balance and clarifies the roles of observation and conversation for different assessment purposes. You'll also explore the role of professional judgment in assessment practices, learn about the teacher-readiness scale, and further explore the benefits of balanced assessment. The chapter concludes with a series of common questions about balanced assessment and key messages to reflect on.

Source: © 2017 by Plan Teach Assess. Used with permission.

Figure 1.1: Observation is part of the balanced assessment to certify drivers.

Balanced Assessment and the VOCAL Approach

We have chosen to call this concept of balanced assessment *VOCAL*, an acronym for *validating observation and conversation when assessing learning*. Clearly, we've selected the VOCAL acronym because it highlights the importance of talk to the assessment process: talk between student and teacher, talk between students themselves, and the talk involving the student, teacher, and parents. That said, we advocate a balanced approach to assessment that involves an appropriate blend of observation, conversation, and student-generated products. *Rebooting Assessment* advocates VOCAL as a way of thinking about and implementing assessment processes that are grounded in sensitive human communication.

The other main argument we are making is that the best way to implement a balanced approach to assessment is to make extensive use of digital technology in all forms: handheld, laptop, desktop, and more. The power of these devices to facilitate communication among stakeholders (teachers, students, and parents) and capture and share in-the-moment evidence of learning as it occurs is a gamechanger for all grade levels. Capturing a conversation between two students as they struggle with a real-world mathematics problem, recording a student reading at key stages of his or her learning, a video recording a lively debate about climate change, and so on—these are all authentic, in-the-moment demonstrations of students' acquisition of essential skills. Students' ability to demonstrate their grasp of important concepts beyond the scope of a written assessment is essential for teachers committed to assessing student proficiency. Figure 1.2 (page 16) illustrates what it looks like for teachers to capture students engaged in performance for the purpose of balanced assessment. Notice how the camera is capturing a record of students' performance while the teacher is in the background using a rubric to capture her own observations.

Validating Observation and Conversation When Assessing Learning

SEE IT

HEAR IT

SHARE IT

ASSESS IT

SAVE IT

Recognize that capturing evidence of student learning in this way doesn't change based on the grade level. Figure 1.3 illustrates how Jackie Clarke, a third-grade teacher at Oodenawi Public School in Oakville, Ontario, employs a rich blend of conversation, performance tasks, and traditional written tasks in order to assess her students' learning. The demonstrations in video 1.1 and video 1.2 show similar approaches at the secondary level. (Note that these links are coded to show just the first forty seconds of each video; the complete videos appear in later chapters.)

Figure 1.3:
Jackie uses conversations and performances as part of her balanced assessment plan.

Video 1.1: Diagnostic Interview

Watch mathematics teacher Jeff Catania conduct a one-to-one interview with Blake, a ninth-grade student who struggles with a traditional assessment task.

Video 1.2: Summative Observation

Watch students in Helen Hills's ninth-grade English language arts (ELA) class engage in a lively discussion of the novel they just read.

Source: © 2017 by Plan Teach Assess. Used with permission.

Now that you have a taste of what balanced assessment can look like, the following sections examine four of its benefits: (1) authenticity, (2) validity, (3) reliability, and (4) differentiation.

Authenticity

When teachers present students with assessment tasks that mimic the world outside of school in an authentic way, they typically become far more engaged and thus produce better work (McTighe, Doubet, & Carbaugh, 2020; Wiggins, 1998). For too many students, proxy measures of learning, such as written tests and examinations, cause anxiety and, consequently, elicit work that does not represent student learning. In core subjects, such as mathematics and science, particularly at the high school level, there has been a historical bias toward using secure, time-bound tests to assess learning at the end of each unit of study. But how often do teachers question their reasons for imposing these constraints? For example, why must all students complete the test within a strict time limit? Why are students prohibited from accessing helpful resources? Why are students denied the opportunity to consult with peers? The same answer applies to all of these questions: to increase reliability. Yes, but is it not true that for some, perhaps many students, these constraints reduce the validity of the evidence gathered? That is to say, while a teacher may be intent upon assessing scientific knowledge, he or she may, in fact, be gathering more evidence about skills associated with efficiency, memorization, and anxiety management.

Whether participating in role playing that requires social interaction, engaging in a debate about climate change, conducting a home audit of waste management, or creating and administering a survey in the community about public transit, students from the early grades through to their senior year of high school benefit from authentic, performance-based assessment tasks. Although many teachers already have their students participate in such tasks as *learning* opportunities, few use such tasks for *assessment* purposes. Many teachers deem performance-based assessments too difficult and too subjective to assess, as compared to written assignments and tests. Traditional performance-based assessments have relied upon teachers' memory, notes, and subjective first impressions of student performance and conversation. However, widespread access to smartphones and tablets with high-quality cameras means teachers and students have in their hands the most powerful assessment tools imaginable (see figure 1.4).

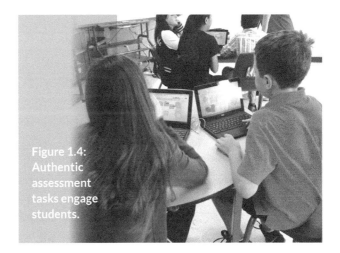

Figure 1.4: Authentic assessment tasks engage students.

Source: © 2017 by Plan Teach Assess. Used with permission.

The pervasiveness of simple-to-use, handheld digital technology means that authentic, performance-based assessment can assume its rightful position as a legitimate, reliable, valid, and engaging way for teachers and students to gather rich evidence of essential learning.

Validity

Validity refers to the confidence teachers have about the inferences they draw from the assessment data they gather relative to targeted learning standards. When teachers choose to use a written test to assess students' skills or competencies, the inferences they draw may be invalid because students' answers are more likely to reflect short-term memorization of facts and procedures rather than proficiency.

Many of the essential skills associated with any and all subject areas are only validly assessed by either talking to students or observing them as they demonstrate their learning. For example, if a learning outcome states, "Students will investigate the interdependence of plants and animals within specific habitats and communities" (Ontario Ministry of Education, 2007a), a written test or report is of questionable validity because the outcome specifically identifies a complex competency. Valid assessment of this learning outcome *demands* that students demonstrate it by *doing*, not writing about it. If teachers instead create an authentic task that provides students with a hands-on opportunity to investigate the interdependence of plants and animals within specific habitats and communities, they can interact with students as they demonstrate learning through research and investigation. Similarly, if teachers want mathematics students to demonstrate mastery of geometry skills (as compared to procedural knowledge of geometry), they need to see students apply their learning to hands-on, authentic geometry problems. And in the humanities, the skills of argumentative discourse are only fully visible when students are required to defend their position, on the fly, in response to an opposing position.

Notice that in each of these examples, the preferred assessment context is dynamic. The demands on students are in a state of flux, requiring agility and flexibility, according to the changing circumstances. The very nature of written assessment is static since the teacher employs a set of predetermined questions. This is not to say there is no place for written evidence of learning. It is necessary, but on its own, it is insufficient as a comprehensive measure of learning, as you read in the example of driver certification at the start of this chapter.

Reliability

Like validity, *reliability* is a measure of the confidence that teachers feel with respect to the conclusions they draw from an assessment. However, *reliability* deals with sampling evidence of learning. No assessment can possibly draw upon all that has been taught and learned within a given instructional cycle. So assessment always involves extracting a sample of evidence of learning and then extrapolating from that sample to draw conclusions about all the learning within the cycle. In attempting to balance efficiency with accuracy of conclusions about learning, teachers need to determine how large the sample of evidence needs to be.

Understanding the principle of *triangulation* is one way for teachers to increase the reliability of their conclusions about students' learning (see figure 1.5). Simply put, teachers should gather at least three pieces of evidence of learning to feel confident about the conclusions they draw (Cooper, 2010; Davies, 2011). While you will explore triangulation in more detail in chapter 2 (page 34), one way to improve balance in your assessment planning is simply to ask, "Have I included opportunities for my students to *do, say, and write*?" In other words, as you create your long-term assessment plans, aim to have students provide evidence of their learning through performance-based assessment and conversation as well as through written work.

This approach to triangulation is, of course, a general guide. For example, many students in grades preK–2 may not be able to write. Hence, most evidence teachers gather will necessarily involve observations and conversations. But for most students in most subject areas, presenting them with three different ways to demonstrate their learning enables teachers to have greater confidence in the conclusions they draw.

Differentiation

For students who struggle with traditional, written forms of assessment, having the opportunity to talk about their learning or demonstrate their learning by *doing* can dramatically reduce anxiety levels and, therefore, result in a more accurate reflection of their learning (Cooper, 2011; Wormeli, 2018). In the introduction (page 1), I wrote about my brother Vince's close call getting into medical school because he struggled to memorize the mountains of science knowledge the examinations demanded at the time. He did not receive the benefits of a differentiated approach to assessment. By contrast, consider Vince's daughter, Kate, who has dyslexia. When it came time for Kate to take her graduation year examinations, her teachers accommodated her needs by using oral exams and allowing her to use a laptop computer to compensate for her difficulty with hand-writing responses to questions. Figure 1.6 illustrates a similar approach with a younger student.

Educational research has led to a much deeper understanding of the different ways students learn and need to be assessed. By ensuring an appropriately balanced approach to assessment that includes conversation and performance, and by making extensive use of handheld

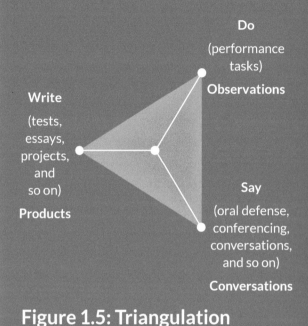

Do (performance tasks)
Observations

Write (tests, essays, projects, and so on)
Products

Say (oral defense, conferencing, conversations, and so on)
Conversations

Figure 1.5: Triangulation of assessment.

Figure 1.6: Differentiation can be as simple as providing a student with a laptop.

Source: © 2017 by Plan Teach Assess. Used with permission.

and other devices to capture evidence of student learning from these forms of assessment, teachers can further differentiate assessment based on how students best show what they know, understand, and can do. In this way, students also feel confident their teachers are gaining a far more reliable picture of their learning.

A Clear Purpose for Assessment

Thus far, we have been discussing balance with respect to using a combination of conversational, performance, and product-based assessment methods. Balance is also of crucial importance when planning assessments according to purpose. Measuring learning at the end of an instructional cycle (summative assessment) has historically received much greater attention from both teachers and parents than assessments designed to improve learning (formative assessment; Chappuis & Stiggins, 2020). In my work, I've found that asking educators to consider different assessment purposes in contexts outside of school can help deepen their understanding of this distinction. To do that, I invite them to consider the figure skater in figure 1.7.

Figure 1.7: Who is assessing this skater affects how they assess the skater.

This skater is performing at a major international competition. A group of judges will score her

performance, and her composite score will determine whether she is on the podium or not at the end of the competition. How did our skater make it to this level? She worked with her coach, perhaps for several years. So who is more invested in the skater's success? The judge or her coach? The coach, of course. So what is the purpose of the judge's assessment of the skater? To evaluate the quality of her final performance.

What is the purpose of the coach's ongoing assessment? To provide feedback to help her excel. What language does the coach use to communicate with the skater during practice? Feedback. What language does the judge use to communicate his evaluation of the skater's performance? A score. Clearly, the coach and judge have very different purposes. Hence, they use different language to communicate.

Returning to the context of schools, the challenge for teachers is to be both coach and judge! So it is essential that teachers be crystal clear themselves as well as when speaking to students and their parents about which hat—coach or judge—they are wearing, when. This leads us to the need to clarify our assessment purpose before we set students to work.

In the following sections, you'll examine several components that lead to having a clear purpose for assessment. We start with a focus on terminology, as there is no common understanding between teachers, students, and parents of an assessment's purpose without shared understanding of the language of assessment.

Reviewing Assessment Terminology

The different terms educators use when talking about assessment can cause a great deal of confusion among colleagues, students, and parents. Similarly, the language educators use to convey what they are assessing can vary, particularly from region to region. For example, many school districts focus on the language of *standards, essential learning, learning targets*, and so on. Others might use *learning intentions* and *success criteria*. For the purposes of this resource, we use the following definitions for frequently used terms and concepts.

- **Learning standards:** The knowledge, concepts, skills, and competencies students are expected to acquire; usually, a state or province authors the learning standards, and they are applicable to all districts and schools.

- **Learning intentions or goals:** The specific knowledge and skills students are expected to acquire, as derived from learning standards; they are often expressed in student-friendly language (unlike state- or province-authored learning standards).

- **Success criteria:** The specific measurable and observable indicators of learning that students are expected to demonstrate

- **Diagnostic (initial or pre-) assessment:** To assess skills, knowledge, and understanding prior to instruction

- **Formative assessment:** To inform learning during the instructional process; this includes both assessment *for* and *as* learning.

- **Common formative assessments:** Team-designed assessments to assess progress toward learning targets, often across a grade level or course

- **Summative assessment:** To assess learning at the end of an instructional period

- **Assessment *as* learning:** Student-monitored assessment to enable progress toward specific learning goals

- **Assessment *for* learning:** To inform learning during the instructional process

- **Assessment *of* learning:** To assess learning at the end of an instructional period

Notice that the definitions for *formative assessment* and *assessment* for *learning* are the same, as are the definitions for *summative assessment* and *assessment* of *learning*. This is deliberate because, respectively, these processes align.

Acknowledging that differences in assessment terminology can overwhelm teachers, we suggest using the following three questions to guide decisions about an assessment's purpose.

1. Is the assessment diagnostic, formative, or summative?

2. Who is the primary user of the resulting assessment data? Teachers? If so, which teachers? The context changes when it's a student's current teacher or a subsequent grade- or course-level teacher, an administrator, and so on. Are the primary users students and parents? An employer? Again, the context for putting assessment data to use changes based on the stakeholder.

3. What kind of data do the primary users need? Do they need feedback? Do they need information about whether students have met specific success criteria on a rubric? Do they need a summative score?

Given that assessment designed to promote learning "is the single most powerful tool we have for both raising standards and empowering lifelong learners" (Broadfoot, Daugherty, Gardner, & Gipps, 1999, p. 2), assessment *for* learning should be where educators put most of their time and energy. Assessment *for* learning includes both diagnostic assessment (also called *initial* or *preassessment*) and formative assessment.

Using Conversations and Performances for Diagnostic Assessment

For teaching to be effective, teachers at all grade levels need to take the time to conduct an initial diagnostic assessment to determine students' current levels of knowledge and skill. Teachers must then use the information they gather through such assessment to determine students' strengths and needs, make decisions about grouping students, ascertain the appropriateness of resources, and make decisions about starting points for instruction. Let's consider, for example, common practice in primary-grade language arts at the beginning of September. To assess students' current reading skills, a teacher conducts a brief reading conference (perhaps five to ten minutes) with each student during the first week of the term (see video 1.3).

Source: © 2017 by Plan Teach Assess. Used with permission.

Each conference might begin with an informal chat to assess the student's attitude toward reading and his or her current reading habits. The teacher may then have the student read a brief grade-level text. We suggest having at least two other texts available—one above grade level and one below—that you can turn to should the student demonstrate his or her reading skills are above or below the grade-level text.

It is just as important for teachers at the high school level to take the time to conduct diagnostic assessment before instruction begins. Many students enter high school reading far below grade level, and unless reading skill deficits are identified and addressed early, the effects of being unable to absorb high school–level content will accumulate over time, often with dire consequences. Teachers of all subject areas should become familiar with the Cloze Procedure (Ellington, 1981), which is an efficient

assessment method for determining the match between core text materials and students' current levels of reading proficiency. The process requires the teacher to select a paragraph of text and delete every fifth word. The assessor then requires students to insert missing words, either with no suggestions provided (basic Cloze) or from an available list of words (modified Cloze). This quickly administered assessment provides teachers with essential information, both with respect to students' prior content knowledge and their knowledge of grammar and syntax.

Using Conversations and Performances for Formative Assessment

Mary James (2017) of the University of Cambridge writes that formative assessment and assessment *for* learning focus on "what is revealed about where children are in their learning, especially the nature of, and reasons for, the strengths and weaknesses they exhibit. Formative judgements are therefore concerned with what they might do to move forward" (p. 4). James (2017) cites the Assessment Reform Group (2002) when defining assessment *for* learning: "Assessment for Learning is the process of seeking and interpreting evidence for use by learners and their teachers to decide where the learners are in their learning, where they need to go and how best to get there" (p. 4).

Depending on the behaviors and maturity of your class, much of the formative evidence of learning can be gathered by students working with peers, capturing evidence of each other's learning using a tablet or smartphone (see figure 1.8).

In video 1.4, Holly Moniz's eighth-grade students use peer assessment to improve their work. They perform a draft version of their infomercial in front of the class. Holly records the performance on each group's tablet while the rest of the class assesses the performance using an online peer-assessment *checkbric* (combination rubric and checklist). Each group then views the recording of their draft

Figure 1.8: Students engaging in online peer assessment.

performance while, at the same time, reading what their peers have said on the checkbric. Groups then discuss how they need to change their infomercials prior to Holly's summative assessment. See chapter 5 (page 104) for a complete case study of Holly's approach.

Your own gathering of formative evidence may occur informally, on the fly, while students engage in learning tasks (see figure 1.9). For example, if students are working in small groups on a science project, move from group to group and ask key questions of individual students to reveal their depth of understanding. You might ask, "Why did you choose to make your observations over several days?" or "How do you know whether the solution was saturated?"

Video 1.4: Group Infomercial Task

Holly's eighth-grade students use peer assessment to improve their work while creating an infomercial they will later perform for the class.

Source: © 2017 by Plan Teach Assess. Used with permission.

Figure 1.9: Holly provides in-the-moment feedback to students.

Source: © 2017 by Plan Teach Assess. Used with permission.

It's About Time

When asked whether the changes she made to her assessment routines take more time, Holly Moniz (personal communication, October 22, 2016) explains:

[Observational formative assessment] involves a shift away from being focused on assessment *of* learning as tangible products. Educators can instead reimagine triangulation of observations and conversations with student work. So it's not about adding time but rather reallocating it and leveraging technology to maximize efficiency.

Google Apps for Education programs, such as Google Keep, Google Docs voice notes, Google Forms, or rubrics in Google Classroom can all be set up to capture in-the-moment assessment. Although these programs take time to learn at first, once they are up and running, it is very quick to include a snapshot of learning within each. For example, with a Google Keep hashtag for each student, a teacher can write a quick digital sticky note capturing a conversation. This can be added to a digital portfolio collection of photos, videos, and sticky notes for this child—essentially created on the go during assessment moments. When it's time to determine a grade, the teacher can simply open up the linked hashtag for the student, and every documented piece completed for him or her throughout the year will come up. Say goodbye to chasing around loose paper and hello to a more balanced assessment portfolio!

Using Conversations and Performances for Summative Assessment

Gathering evidence of learning for summative purposes involves certifying students' proficiency and understanding according to clear performance standards. In the immortal words of the late Grant Wiggins, teachers will use such evidence to "convict students of learning" (G. Wiggins, personal communication, November 1993). In other words, the burden of proof for what students learned is higher than when assessing diagnostically or formatively.

Remember, summative assessment involves certifying the proficiency of students with respect to learning intentions at the end of an instructional period. Well-designed summative assessment tasks embed the broad, overall learning outcomes that represent essential learning in a given strand. The level of performance a student demonstrates on a summative assessment will indicate whether or not that student is prepared to handle similar work at the next grade level. As such, summative assessment involves higher stakes than other forms of assessment. To return to a previous analogy, summative assessment is the equivalent of the in-car road test required for driver certification. Too often, in the middle and senior grades, summative assessment takes the form of secure, timed, and written tests—an assessment method that places many students at risk. The VOCAL approach sees teachers exploring alternatives to this format.

For example, Stephanie Girvan teaches mathematics at Dr. Frank J. Hayden Secondary School in Burlington, Ontario. Many of the students in her eleventh-grade workplace mathematics course struggle with the work and have significant gaps in their mathematics learning. As a result, Stephanie finds being flexible in her approach by offering students the option of an oral final assessment provides deeper insights into students' acquired learning (see video 1.5).

Video 1.5: A Flexible Approach to Summative Assessment

Stephanie uses a conversation-based format to summatively assess a student in a workplace mathematics course.

The Role of Professional Judgment

You may notice in video 1.5 that Stephanie finds it necessary to probe the student's knowledge and understanding in ways unique to that student. This is a *professional judgment* call on her part (Allal, 2013), meaning Stephanie must rely upon her own knowledge base with respect to the mathematics involved, her specific experience in working with each of her students, and her understanding of sound assessment practice to ensure that the evidence of learning she gathers meets acceptable standards of reliability and validity. In this example, Stephanie's approach has the potential to reduce the reliability of the information she gathers relative to other students in the class who participate in a more conventional written assessment. To control for this potential source of bias, Stephanie has at her fingertips a standard set of prompts that she uses when the need arises. She keeps a record of which prompts she uses with each student since these represent scaffolding required to elicit student responses. Her grading will reflect the amount of scaffolding required for each student. There are no hard-and-fast rules about how much or how little a teacher should prompt a student. Teachers must strike the appropriate balance between expecting the student to respond independently and providing nudges when they suspect students understand the material but require some prompting (see figure 1.10, page 26). Ultimately, especially in the senior grades, teachers should expect students to

> *Whereas U.S. tests rely primarily on multiple-choice items that evaluate recall and recognition of discrete facts, most high-achieving countries rely largely on open-ended items that require students to analyze, apply knowledge, and write extensively. Furthermore, their growing emphasis on project-based, inquiry-oriented learning has led to an increasing prominence for school-based tasks, which include research projects, science investigations, development of products, and reports or presentations about these efforts. (Darling-Hammond & McCloskey, 2008, p. 264)*

demonstrate proficiency on essential learning with little or no support. (Note that *support* refers to subject-based knowledge, understanding, and skills. Students with identified special learning needs may expect to receive accommodations—for as long as necessary.)

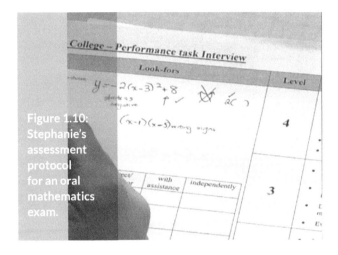

Figure 1.10: Stephanie's assessment protocol for an oral mathematics exam.

Pause and Reflect

- What are the possible advantages of conducting a summative interview instead of a written test?

- What do you see as the implications of using summative interviews with respect to determining final grades and reporting to parents?

What Is Being Assessed?

In discussions with teachers and school administrators over many years, we've noticed they often use the terms *growth*, *progress*, and *achievement* interchangeably. These are, in fact, three distinctly different ways to summarize student learning (Wiggins, 1998).

1. **Growth:** Growth is a measure of change over the elapsed time. It requires at least two data points: (1) before instruction begins and (2) at the end of an instructional cycle. However, while teachers may compare growth to normative trends such as a growth continuum for reading skills acquisition, there is not a specific and firm expectation with regard to how much change occurs by the end of the instructional cycle. (For that, see *progress*.) Think of measuring the growth of the human body where, except in cases of a height requirement (such as when accessing an amusement park ride), whatever height an individual attains, others deem acceptable.

2. **Progress:** Assessing progress is different from growth in that although *progress* also requires at least two data points (again, pre- and post-instruction), teachers measure the change over time according to progress toward an expected performance level. Think of measuring driving distance, when travelers determine progress toward a given destination.

3. **Achievement:** *Achievement* is simply a single measure of performance at a moment in time. Unlike measures of growth and progress, achievement is not concerned with change over time as a result of instruction. It is common for grades at different reporting periods throughout the academic year to simply be discrete measures of achievement. One of the most harmful consequences of schools focusing exclusively on achievement is that students, teachers, and especially parents come to believe there are *A students*, *B students*, and *C students*. Since such labels become inextricably linked with levels of motivation and self-esteem, they can lead to fixed mindsets of everyone involved.

In early childhood contexts, given preschoolers of differing backgrounds and home experiences, teachers often use growth continua to allow for the wide variation in prior knowledge and skills that children bring to school. These continua, which chart the typical path very young students demonstrate as they acquire essential skills, allow for a wider range of performance within a given grade. The VOCAL approach advocates gathering evidence of student *growth* over time by engaging in conversations and observing performances with these young learners and their parents.

Source: © 2017 by Plan Teach Assess. Used with permission.

It is common and acceptable practice for measures of growth to merge with measures of progress over time as children move from the primary grades (preK to grade 3) into the junior grades (4–6). This is a necessary transition since school systems are predicated on the expectation that most students will reach essential benchmarks within a specified period of time in core areas such as language arts, mathematics, science, and the social sciences. For example, students are expected to progress toward clearly identified levels of reading proficiency by the end of specified grade levels. That said, in conversations with parents throughout the year, and particularly following a reporting period, teachers should focus discussions on students' visible learning gains over time relative to learning intentions. Doing so will go some way toward challenging the mindset among some educators that a student is born "bright," "average," or "dull" or the mindset of a parent who insists, "This grade can't be right. My child is an A student."

The Teacher-Readiness Scale

Consider for a moment your current comfort level in terms of balanced assessment and using digital technology to assess student learning. If you haven't approached assessment in this way up to this point, the kinds of changes to your practice this resource presents may represent a significant challenge. Hence, we have differentiated implementation options based on your current familiarity with balanced assessment and the use of digital technology for assessment purposes. The Teacher-Readiness Scale in figure 1.11 (page 28) identifies the following four levels of skill and familiarity.

1. **Curiosity:** I'm curious to learn about. . . .
2. **Commitment:** I'm taking steps and beginning to. . . .
3. **Capacity:** I'm building on my knowledge and skills for . . . .
4. **Confirmation:** I'm proficient at and helping others to. . . .

You can apply these levels collaboratively as you interact with your teaching colleagues, citing personal examples of what you are trying in the classroom (see figure 1.12, page 29). Examine the complete teacher-readiness scale in figure 1.11 to identify your current skill and knowledge levels with respect to balanced assessment. You may wish to print a copy of the scale and highlight the indicators that best match where you are. Expect to find yourself confident in some areas and less confident in others.

As you progress through this resource, you will find the Shift and Share feature that suggests actions and implementation strategies. These are matched to the four levels on the teacher-readiness scale to help you select an appropriate level of challenge for you and your colleagues. Be sure to view your place on the scale as dynamic, moving yourself from one level to the next as you gain confidence and hone your skills.

	Curiosity *"I'm curious to learn about . . ."*	**Commitment** *"I'm taking steps and beginning to . . ."*	**Capacity** *"I'm building on my knowledge and skills for . . ."*	**Confirmation** *"I'm proficient at, and helping others to . . ."*
Why should I balance the way I assess student learning?	Why observations of student performance and evidence from conversations might improve the quality and effectiveness of my assessment practice	Explore ways to use observations of student performance and evidence from conversations as part of my assessment practice	Using observations of student performance and evidence from conversations as part of my assessment practice	Use student observations and conversations to improve the quality and effectiveness of their assessment practice
How can digital technology help?	Why technology may or may not have a role in my assessment of student performances and conversations	Collaborate with colleagues who have more expertise to learn to use technology to capture evidence of student performance and conversation	Using technology to capture evidence of student performance and conversation	Use technology to gather, share, and manage evidence of observations and conversations
How do I plan balanced assessment?	Developing assessment plans that include observations and conversations	Develop assessment plans that include evidence from observations and conversations	Developing assessment plans that reflect an appropriate balance of written, oral, and performance evidence	Design assessment plans that include a purposeful balance of written, oral, and performance evidence
How do I assess learning using balanced assessment?	At least one simple way to gather evidence through observations and conversations	Gather evidence of learning through observations and conversations	Gathering evidence through observations and conversations	Gather, share, and involve students in assessing evidence through observations and conversations
How do I use digital technology to implement balanced assessment?	How to watch and assess student performances or interviews live without technology	Allow students to use technology to capture evidence of their learning	Using cloud technology to capture, share, and manage evidence of students' learning	Use technology in a variety of ways to capture evidence of students' learning
How do I support students in curating and sharing their own learning using digital evidence?	How to help students capture evidence from observations and conversations to improve communication with teachers and parents about their learning	Require students to select and review evidence from observations and conversations to improve communication with teachers and parents about their learning	Supporting students in presenting and sharing evidence from observations and conversations to improve communication with teachers and parents about their learning	Enable students to become independent and effective assessors of their own learning and communicating this to others through ePortfolios
How do I use balanced assessment to improve learning?	How to use evidence from observations and conversations with students to help them improve their learning	Use evidence from observations and conversations with students to help them improve their learning	Using evidence from observations and conversations with students to help them improve their learning	Use evidence from observations and conversations with students to help them improve their learning
How do I communicate about learning using digital evidence?	How to use evidence from observations and conversations to improve my communication with parents about their children's learning	Use evidence from observations and conversations to improve my communication with parents about their children's learning	Using evidence from observations and conversations to improve my communication with parents about their children's learning	Use evidence from observations and conversations to improve their communication with parents about their children's learning

Figure 1.11: The Teacher-Readiness Scale.

*Visit **go.SolutionTree.com/assessment** for a free reproducible version of this figure.*

Figure 1.12: Collaboration is key to implementing change.

Questions About Balanced Assessment

The following sections address common questions we hear from teachers about balanced assessment.

What Are Students and Teachers Saying About Balanced Assessment?

During our work with those teachers who have embraced the use of conversation and performance-based assessment, along with the use of digital technology for capturing evidence of learning, we have observed the following common key features.

- A sense of excitement, enthusiasm, and joy of learning that is apparent among both students and teachers

- Deep levels of engagement with the work, from primary classrooms through to senior high school, as evidenced by time on task, perseverance, and self-efficacy

- An almost complete absence of discipline problems within the classroom

Our hope is that by reading *Rebooting Assessment*, an ever-increasing number of educators will be able to learn from the teachers and students featured and, thereby, share in these positive changes. View

video 1.6 to listen to students and teachers talk about the value of assessment through observation and conversation.

Notice from video 1.6 that using conversations and performance-based observations impacts both Jackie and her students. You see and hear students affirm, "It's just a better way. I am more of an oral person" and, "I like it because you kind of like get a chance to discuss it first and figure out what you are going to say" (Rebooting Assessment, 2021a). Jackie affirms these sentiments when she says:

> Kids have so much to share. When it comes to pencil and paper, they only give me a limited amount, and I just feel that there is so much more inside of kids that we can tap into if we just ask, and we talk and share. (Rebooting Assessment, 2021a)

Video 1.6: The Value of the VOCAL Approach
Students and teachers discuss the value of balanced assessment.

Source: © 2017 by Plan Teach Assess. Used with permission.

Jackie further details how much more she learns from her students than she would from using only a pencil-and-paper assessment, as students feel compelled to explain their thinking in more detail instead of just writing a quick sentence or two that don't convey their full understanding. Jackie sums up the experience best by saying:

> I just feel that when you look at those couple of sentences they wrote to you, there is some great stuff in there, of course. But have the kids defended it? Could you prompt further? Were there directions I could have taken

their learning? I just feel that with tests and short-answer questions, they give you an answer for sure, you can get a mark for the report card, but it doesn't help you develop your kids. (Rebooting Assessment, 2021a)

To help you assess your own perspective on balanced assessment, use the Shift and Share in figure 1.13 to determine next steps. Note that this and similar figures omit a curiosity-level application as all teachers can begin from this stage without additional guidance.

Why Is Technology Such a Game Changer?

The increasing availability of camera-ready devices provides a solution to a problem that has hindered assessment reform for years—the perceived subjectivity of performance-based assessment. Using video capture, teachers and students can quickly and easily create a permanent in-the-moment digital record of *growth, progress,* or *achievement* that is simple to store, review, reassess, and share with all

What is your current level of familiarity with balanced assessment? Self-assess using the following section of the teacher-readiness scale. Consider taking one step to the right of where you are comfortable as a next step for your practice.

	Curiosity "I'm curious to learn about . . . ."	Commitment "I'm taking steps and beginning to . . . ."	Capacity "I'm building on my knowledge and skills for . . . ."	Confirmation "I'm proficient at, and helping others to . . . ."
Why should I balance the way I assess student learning?	Why observations of student performance and evidence from conversations might improve the quality and effectiveness of my assessment practice	Explore ways to use observations of student performance and evidence from conversations as part of my assessment practice	Using observations of student performance and evidence from conversations as part of my assessment practice	Use student observations and conversations to improve the quality and effectiveness of their assessment practice

Commitment-Level Application

Initiate a chat with teachers in your school about balanced assessment. How much do they value formative assessment compared to summative assessment? What practices do they currently use that rely on observations of performance and conversation to assess learning?

Capacity-Level Application

Review the classroom video clips in this chapter, and decide what strategies other teachers use that you could incorporate into your own practice. What changes or adjustments would you make to suit your curriculum and students?

Confirmation-Level Application

Invite colleagues, either in person or online, to join you in researching ways to make greater use of assessment through performance observation and conversation in your classrooms. Commit to sharing your collective learning over the course of a term and using that acquired knowledge to further improve your use of balanced assessment.

Figure 1.13: Shift and Share—Balanced assessment readiness.

Visit go.SolutionTree.com/assessment for a free reproducible version of this figure.

stakeholders, from colleagues to students and parents. (You'll learn more about this in chapter 6, page 126.) For example, a teacher might use her tablet to capture brief samples of each student reading at key points during the school year in order to track progress toward learning intentions, adjust her instructional plans as needed to support each student's unique needs, and share with parents their child's learning (see figure 1.14).

Figure 1.14: Jackie conducts a reading conference and captures it on a tablet.

Source: © 2017 by Plan Teach Assess. Used with permission.

How Do I Convince Parents of the Value of Balanced Assessment?

Think about how pervasive assessment through observation is in our lives outside of school. Maybe you play golf? If so, I'll bet lessons you've taken involved video analysis of your swing. Have you been to a hockey, football, or soccer game lately? Rest assured, the coaches and players spent hours viewing video footage of previous games to help improve the team's play. Even the Royal Conservatory of Music in Toronto, Ontario, makes extensive use of student video performance, both to instruct and to celebrate excellence.

These everyday examples can help parents come to appreciate the potential of using video in schools to observe and digitally capture a student's performance and then provide feedback to support subsequent performance improvements. Share with parents these examples, and then ask, "So why wouldn't we use video in school to let you see your child's learning as it occurs?"

The important thing is not to assume that we have to forget everything that is known about assessment and feedback just because we now have technology. . . . What we know about validity, reliability, transparency and authenticity of assessment still applies. We have to . . . uphold all of those values, but also use the new tools appropriately.

(Joint Information Systems Committee [JISC], 2020, p. 55)

It's About Time

At this point in your reading, you may be thinking, "All these changes will surely add to the time I already spend on assessment." But as Holly commented earlier, rather than more time for assessment, consider a balanced approach to assessment as *reallocation of time*. For example, many teachers believe they are the only assessors in the classroom. But by making effective use of recording devices, teachers empower students to become highly effective self-assessors of their own learning (Van der Kleij, Adie, & Cumming, 2017). Teachers should aim to have all students become reliable, autonomous assessors of their own performance and independent adjusters of their own performance. Doing so can dramatically reduce the time teachers spend on assessment and remediation. Furthermore, by pairing recording technology with increasing access to high-quality software and apps for sharing, reviewing, and discussing (including communicating feedback and grades), those recordings mean a critical piece for using conversations and performances with students for assessment purposes is in place.

And what about conversation? When teachers listen to students engaged in conversations related to their learning, they literally see into students' thinking. They learn about students' levels of understanding, their misconceptions, their tolerance for other perspectives and points of view, their ability to listen to and build on the ideas of others, and their ability to answer questions. Note all this to parents, and ask, "Will a written test enable me to see your child's ability to demonstrate these things?"

It's also worth reflecting on the idea that the younger the students, the easier it typically is for teachers to convince parents about the value of assessing based on conversations and performances. When students haven't yet acquired foundational reading and writing skills, parents expect teachers to use conversation and performance-based observation in assessing growth and progress. The challenge is to convince parents of older children that balanced assessment is valid, reliable, and essential in all grades. More on that issue in chapter 6 (page 126). You'll also find a sample parent communication explaining the benefits of balanced assessment in the appendix (page 153).

Key Messages

As you reflect on this chapter, we urge you to focus on the following
key messages.

1. As educators prepare students for life beyond school, they must be willing to
   examine how assessment practices need to change in order to provide students
   with the information they need to deepen learning and improve communication
   with parents about what their children are learning.

2. A balanced approach to assessment includes gathering evidence of learning
   by observing students as they demonstrate skills and engaging them in
   conversation to assess understanding, as well as collecting written work and
   other learning products.

3. Balanced assessment also means that teachers achieve an appropriate blend
   of diagnostic, formative, and summative assessment data to differentiate
   instruction, maximize learning, and certify proficiency at the end of an
   instructional cycle.

4. Triangulation is a crucial guiding principle when planning a balanced approach to
   assessment.

5. Determining your own comfort level with balanced assessment and technology is
   an essential first step to implementation.

6. The benefits of balanced assessment include greater authenticity, validity,
   reliability, and differentiation.

7. Smartphones and tablets are your most valuable tools when implementing
   balanced assessment.

8. Some parents may need convincing that balanced assessment is more effective
   than traditional forms of assessment.

CHAPTER 2

How Do I Plan for Balanced Assessment?

When I began my teaching career, I used a curriculum planning template that comprised four columns: (1) objectives, (2) instructional strategies, (3) resources, and (4) evaluation. I was conscientious in completing the first three columns for each course that I was going to teach. But the fourth column I left blank, rationalizing, "How do I know what work I'm going to evaluate until I've done the teaching?" How my thinking was to change in later years! As you shall see later in this chapter, sound curriculum and course planning begin with the end in mind. Having first identified essential learning targets, the very next question teachers address must be, "What summative assessments must I use to elicit evidence that students have met these targets?" The nature of each learning target will point to the need for assessment to occur through conversation, performance, product, or a combination of these modes.

Stop for a moment to consider how much you learn about a colleague you've just met by listening to what they say and observing their actions. Your ears and eyes record huge amounts of information, which your brain then processes to assess the individual's knowledge, interests, beliefs, personality, and potential for compatibility (Schiller, Freeman, Mitchell, Uleman, & Phelps, 2009). Observation and conversation are vital assessment strategies in educators' day-to-day lives, and teachers need to view them as such in the context of formal teaching and learning. However, because conventional assessment strategies beyond the primary grades tend to rely on traditional written products, teachers typically ask, "What kinds of things should I observe?" and "What kinds of conversations would I assess?" While there are no hard-and-fast rules governing decisions about which assessment mode to use (conversation, performance, or product), a combination of the guidelines in this chapter, coupled with your intuition as an educator, will ensure you plan an appropriate balance.

In this chapter, you'll learn more about using triangulation to improve assessment reliability, how and when to observe and converse, and how to use backward planning to achieve a balanced and efficient assessment portfolio.

Triangulation of Assessment Evidence

Triangulation, which simply means you need three data points to accurately locate a specific place or generate a set of directions, is a way to increase the likelihood that conclusions you draw from a data set are reliable (Cooper, 2010; Davies, 2011). Triangulation is a strategy humans have used throughout history to pinpoint their location. Modern Global Positioning System (GPS) devices rely on triangulation by satellite (technically *trilateration*) to provide locations and directions (Lartaud, 2015).

In the context of student assessment, your goal is to *locate* where students are with respect to learning *destinations*. Notice how these same geographical terms are equally appropriate to assessment (see figure 2.1, page 36). Diagnostic assessment seeks to determine *where* students are as they begin their learning *journey*; formative assessment provides information about *how far* the student has *traveled* and how much further they need to go; and summative assessment confirms whether or not students have reached their *destination*.

The similarities between GPS and assessment don't end here; both require data. In the assessment context, and in figure 2.2 (page 36), for teachers to have confidence about their conclusions, they should gather at least three data points about each student's learning (Boudett, City, & Murnane, 2013).

**Figure 2.1:
Triangulation of data is common
to both GPS and high-quality
assessment systems.**

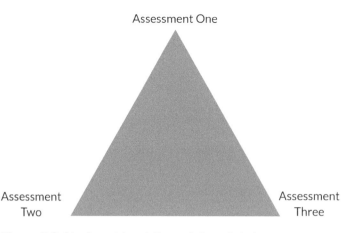

Figure 2.2: Having at least three data points improves
assessment reliability.

Whether the learning goal is reading fluency, long division, civic responsibility, perspective drawing, engaging in debate, or any other curriculum content, teachers need a minimum of three pieces of data.

Teachers have long realized the need to have students answer multiple questions dealing with a specific concept or procedure in order to reach reliable conclusions about their depth of understanding. One question answered correctly may be unreliable. Two answers, one correct and one incorrect, are inconclusive. But answers to three questions enable teachers to determine the *mode*, or the most consistent level. Note that *mode* has two meanings. Statistically, *mode* means the most frequently occurring number, but it also refers to the type of assessment used: performance task, conversation, or student product. Clearly, having students answer more than three questions can further improve reliability, but teachers must strike a manageable balance between reliability and efficiency.

A second way to triangulate assessment is by assessment mode (type). To *triangulate by assessment mode* means ensuring that students have opportunities to demonstrate their learning in three ways: (1) conversations, (2) performance tasks that teachers observe, and (3) tangible products. A simple way to remember this, as you read about in the Reliability section (see page 18 in chapter 1), is having students *do*, *write*, and *say*. Figure 2.3 combines the triangulation concepts in figure 1.5 (page 19) and figure 2.2 to show how triangulation by mode has the potential to increase the validity of the inferences teachers make about student learning.

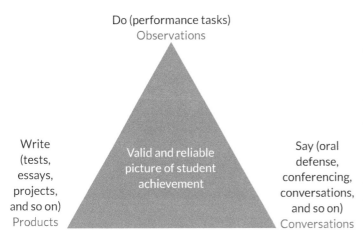

Figure 2.3: Triangulation of assessments by mode.

While it is typical for elementary teachers to gather a variety of evidence of learning that includes conversations, performances, and products, we find such practice less pervasive in high schools. Secondary teachers can increase their confidence in end-of-course grade determinations by ensuring they have product, performance, and oral evidence of student proficiency. For example, a science teacher may want to ensure final grades are based on students' skills as demonstrated during a final lab experiment, a brief one-to-one conference in which the teacher probes each student's understanding of key concepts, as well as a representative sample of lab reports. In this case, looking at the mode means looking at the most consistent level of achievement across three types of evidence: (1) an observed performance, (2) an oral explanation, and (3) a set of products.

Questions About Planning Assessments

The following sections address common questions we hear from teachers about planning for balanced assessments.

How Much Observing and Conversing Do I Need to Do?

A shortage of instructional time, as well as the teacher's energy level, will limit how much assessment through observation and conversation actually occurs. That said, teachers must turn again to their assessment plan, remembering that students can carry out much of the formative assessment themselves. In the spirit of *backward design*—that is, beginning with the end in mind (McTighe & Curtis, 2019)—the first question to ask yourself is, "How much summative evidence do I need to gather to conclude, with confidence, that a student has demonstrated mastery on a given set of learning intentions and success criteria?" Once again, the principle of triangulation should be your guide. Hence, the answer is a minimum of three samples.

Let's say that you want to determine a student's oral reading fluency at the end of a term (see figure 2.4, page 38). Three oral reading samples occurring at different times, using three different, previously unseen texts, will comprise a valid sample of summative evidence (see figure 2.5, page 38).

With respect to gathering *diagnostic* assessment data—data to determine students' prior knowledge and skill levels before instruction begins—the principle of balanced assessment should again apply. That is, don't rely on one assessment task to assess strengths and gaps in learning, especially if that task is a written quiz. For example, you may intend to assess science knowledge, but if a student incorrectly answers a quiz question, that may reflect a lack of understanding of the question or how to compose a written answer. In short, the question ends up assessing literacy rather than scientific knowledge.

Using observation and conversation in addition to a written quiz enables you to triangulate. For this example, you might assign a simple scientific investigation in which students answer a series of questions about the environment adjacent to your school. Prior to having students complete a simple written quiz (on their return to class), observe

Figure 2.4: Students read independently while the teacher conducts a reading conference.

Source: © 2017 by Plan Teach Assess. Used with permission.

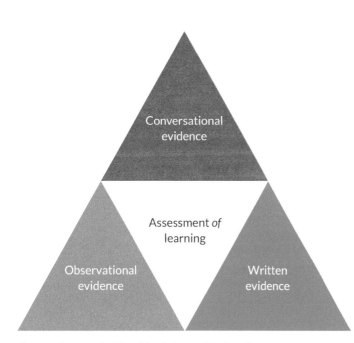

Source: © 2017 by Plan Teach Assess. Used with permission.

Figure 2.5: Gather evidence to certify proficiency and understanding.

them as they conduct the investigation and ask questions, probing what they are doing during the investigation.

By contrast, most early childhood (preK–2) assessment, out of necessity, involves observation and conversation. For example, if the learning goal is *collaboration*, focused observation and conversation during the first few weeks of term provide teachers with the data they need about each student's prior learning in this area.

The answer to how much formative assessment information you need to gather is not simple. It depends on individual students. Think of coaching youth soccer: How much time does the coach need to spend observing players to make sound decisions about who needs practice shooting, dribbling, passing, and so on? How much practice does each player need with these respective skills? It depends on the skills he or she brings to the field. As a general principle, the lower a student's skill level for a specific task, the more formative assessment teachers should gather to plan appropriate instruction for that student.

When Is It Most Beneficial to Assess Learning Through Student-Generated Products?

When we speak about products to be assessed, we mean tangible pieces of writing such as reports, term papers, creative writing, letters, and journals. Products also include research projects, pieces of art, dioramas, and scale models. Products may be oral in nature, such as prepared drama productions and oral presentations. When teachers are developing an assessment plan, they need to think of these products as summative, polished pieces of work that facilitate the assessment of a cluster of learning outcomes (figure 2.6). Effective assessment planning then sees teachers working backward from these polished pieces, enabling students and teachers to work together through the formative process in which students master smaller sub-parts of the whole.

Products are artifacts students generate to demonstrate they have met pre-specified criteria having to do with design, quality, performance, and impact. Granted, there are typically numerous opportunities for the assessment of skills and work habits during the creation of products. So it is often appropriate and desirable to specify both *process* and *product* assessment criteria. This distinction is crucial when several students collaborate in the creation

It's About Time

Because rates of learning differ, it is rarely, if ever, the case that all students are equipped for success on summative assessment tasks at the same time. Consequently, teachers face constant tension between the fixed time frame (that is, the traditional academic term or year) and the reality that different students learn at different rates. When teachers use written tests as their preferred method for summative assessment, as a matter of fairness, they often feel compelled to have all students complete the test at the same time, particularly if those tests focus on recall of content knowledge. But when summative assessments focus on demonstration of competencies and involve recording conversations and performance tasks, it is no longer necessary to have all students complete the assessments at the same time, simply because there is no need for test security.

Figure 2.6:
Students work on the initial stage of a summative task.

of a single product—for example, a scale model of a self-propelled car. The model car must be assessed according to the extent to which it meets a set of design and performance criteria. But the students who worked to produce the car must each be assessed on their demonstration of the design, problem-solving, and collaborative skills required to be an effective member of the team. So the teacher may choose to assess these individual skills by observing students as they work in their teams while also engaging individual students in brief conversations while they work. The teacher may schedule more in-depth conversations outside of the hands-on work time. This example illustrates the fact that rich assessment is rarely limited to a single mode: a product, a performance, or a conversation. Well-designed rich assessment tasks typically integrate two or more of these modes.

When Is It Most Beneficial to Assess Learning Through Observation of Performance?

The simple answers to this question are:

1. When assessing skills and competencies

2. When assessment is formative

3. When students struggle with traditional assessment formats

The following sections address each of these opportunities.

Assessing Skills and Competencies

Assessment through conversations and performances is necessary when learning outcomes involve skills and competencies—in fact, it is essential. While this has always been apparent to teachers of physical education, drama, and the trades, teachers in traditional academic subjects—mathematics, English language arts (ELA), and the social sciences—often focus on the assessment of products.

"Now, wait a minute," a high school mathematics teacher says. "I'm assessing skills when my students write a chapter test." While this is true, written tests are, by their very nature, static products. In creating the test, teachers decide what the questions are and the constraints of the testing environment—usually a time limit; there is no opportunity to collaborate and no access to relevant resources. These constraints are what render the task *static*. But ask yourself: "How many mathematics problems do I find myself solving as an adult that are static, timed, autonomous, and deny me access to resources?" Most problems people face in their lives are dynamic, fluid, ill-defined, and inevitably require consultation with others (see figure 2.7). Why shouldn't high school mathematics look like this roller coaster–themed problem?

A new theme park is in the planning and design stages. You are one of the project engineers, leading a team that is designing a roller coaster. While it must be safe, the ride must also give riders a thrilling freefall feeling. You are to prepare a computerized design of the profile of the roller coaster. Begin by designing the ride on graph paper. However, your final design must include the mathematical models needed to redraw the profile of the ride using a graphing calculator or graphing software. (Zimmer et al., 2001, p. 243)

Figure 2.7: Authentic performance tasks engage students and thereby provide rich evidence of learning.

This authentic performance task is truly dynamic: it has no single, correct answer; it demands critical-thinking and problem-solving skills; and it requires students to access a great deal of previously acquired learning and apply it in a novel way.

Assessment through observation is critical when the focus is determining how well students respond to *problem-solving tasks*—tasks that are messy, fluid, and do not have a single correct solution. For example, Jeff Boulton teaches Mathematics and Economics at Iroquois Ridge High School in Oakville, Ontario. In his senior economics class, at the end of the semester, students participate in a five-day simulation called *G7*, a recording of which is available as part of a companion DVD with *Talk About Assessment: High School Strategies and Tools* (Cooper, 2010). Working in small groups that each represent one of the G7 countries, Jeff expects students to apply their learning from the course while trading and negotiating with other countries in an effort to maximize economic benefits for their own country (see figure 2.8). During the course, he ensures his students acquire all the knowledge, skills, and understanding required to participate successfully in the simulation. He also plans all the formative assessments to scaffold students' learning in preparation for the summative simulation.

Throughout the G7 simulation, Jeff gathers much of his richest assessment data as he observes and listens to group members negotiating, compromising, demanding, and cajoling as they interact with other countries' delegates.

Figure 2.8: Students negotiating in the interests of their respective countries during a G7 simulation.

Assessing Formatively

Conversations and performance-based observations are critical during the formative stage of learning. Unfortunately, many high school courses feature a *teach-test-move on model* in which some students find themselves writing end-of-unit tests long before they have acquired the necessary learning to be successful. Understandably, this situation is a consequence of organizing schools and defining learning not in terms of individual student mastery of learning but according to the number of hours students spend

at their desks. It stands to reason that if the time to learn is held constant for a class full of students, then achievement must vary, with some students not acquiring essential learning. I write in detail about this problem in *Talk About Assessment: High School Strategies and Tools* (Cooper, 2010), and it's a key concept in the professional learning community (PLC) process (DuFour, DuFour, Eaker, Many, & Mattos, 2016).

For now, suffice to say, formative assessment is crucial in determining students' readiness to complete summative tasks. Since formative assessment must focus on gaps in learning rather than the learning students have mastered, the teacher's response to data derived from such assessment must be flexible. Different students will demonstrate different gaps in their learning and will, therefore, require differentiated responses from the teacher. Interacting with and observing students as they engage with learning reveal rich data about their preparedness—or lack thereof—for summative assessment. After all, would you register to take your in-car driving test if you didn't feel ready?

Assessing Students Who Struggle With Traditional Assessment Formats

For students who struggle with written tests, observing them as they demonstrate their *learning by doing* can provide a far more accurate picture of their skills and understanding. Consider Jack, a fourth-grade student who has just completed a written test about rocks and minerals. Jack failed the test. After consulting Jack's student record, Mr. Brooks (his teacher), is reminded that Jack is reading at a first-grade level. However, the test included words far above that level, such as *igneous*, *sedimentary*, and *metamorphic*. In reality, this wasn't a science test for Jack, it was a reading test, and Jack was already receiving separate interventive instruction to accelerate his reading skills to grade level.

Concerned about the validity of the test score, Mr. Brooks sits down with Jack and says, "Jack, I'm pretty sure you know plenty about rocks and minerals, especially since you were so interested when we went on the field trip to the quarry. So let's have a chat, and you can show and tell me what you know."

Using rock and mineral samples, Mr. Brooks helps Jack recall his fascination during the field trip, as well as during class when students examined the properties of similar samples. Throughout the chat, Mr. Brooks captures with his tablet's video camera evidence of Jack's knowledge and understanding of unit concepts, including his correct use of the terms *igneous*, *sedimentary*, and *metamorphic*. By not taking the written test result at face value and seeking another source of evidence that involved observation and conversation, Mr. Brooks was able to gather valid evidence of Jack's learning for the class's *science* curriculum.

It is important to note that in his chat with Jack, Mr. Brooks maintains the same degree of scientific rigor as the written test questions. That is to say, while he made the accommodation of having Jack respond to the questions orally, he maintained the same level of complexity as the written test demands. This is crucial to avoid the common problem of "dumbing down" an assessment task when accommodations are made for a student with special needs.

When Is It Most Beneficial to Assess Learning Through Conversations?

The example of Jack and Mr. Brooks in the previous section illustrates that assessment through conversation is quite distinct from common forms of oral assessment. It's common for teachers to rely on oral presentations to assess learning. However, such presentations are often contrived and rehearsed, and individual or group tasks consume huge amounts of instructional time, rarely engage those who are not presenting, and bear scant resemblance to authentic tasks outside school. The happiest students in the class have surnames that begin with *A* since they often get to go first, "get to say stuff for the first time, rather than repeat what everyone else has said," and "get to slack off for the rest of the week," listening to all the other presentations.

Assessment through conversation is entirely different. It requires students to speak extemporaneously. They must rely on their knowledge and understanding to explain with clarity, convince others of their views, listen and respond to impromptu questions, think on the fly, and encourage, question, challenge, summarize, and synthesize—all in a dynamic, fluid, and unrehearsed way. All of this we see in Helen Hills's ninth-grade ELA class (see figure 2.9).

Figure 2.9: Helen's ninth-grade ELA novel seminar.

Source: © 2017 by Plan Teach Assess. Used with permission.

Or, consider a traditional science fair, something I often participated in as an external judge. My task was to examine and assess students' various group products, which I hoped had been completed with minimal parent intervention! To improve *inter-rater reliability*—different assessors coming to similar conclusions about student work—(Phelan & Wren, 2005–2006)—the judges usually received a rubric identifying certain design criteria. For me, the most telling assessment occurred when I asked individual students questions such as the following.

- "How does water purity affect surface tension?"

- "Which material is the best insulator?"

- "How does arch curvature affect load-carrying strength?"

- "How do different foundations stand up to earthquakes?"

Students' ability to respond successfully to such questions is a very good indicator of their depth of learning. Only by engaging these budding scientists in conversation was I able to get beyond the sometimes superficial evidence of learning reflected in the products they displayed at the science fair.

Similarly, when teachers engage in conversations with students, they model the metacognitive and assessment skills necessary for self- and peer assessment. For example, Jackie Clarke, whom we introduced you to in chapter 1 (page 12), couldn't

imagine assessing her third-grade students' reading skills without relying on observations of each student's performance and one-to-one conversations with each student (see figure 2.10). You'll find a complete case study illustrating Jackie's approach in chapter 5 (page 104).

What Is the Appropriate Balance of Conversations, Performances, and Products?

There is no formula for achieving an appropriate balance of assessment methods. Rich assessments typically involve two or more modes. When teachers make a long-range assessment plan, they must begin with the curriculum. Examining the set of learning outcomes for a given subject and grade level or for a specific course, teachers must determine which clusters of outcomes they can best assess primarily through products, which clusters require observation, and which clusters lend themselves to assessment through conversation.

Learning outcomes for a given curriculum can include a variety of domains: knowledge, conceptual understanding, cognitive skills, competencies, and even attitudes and behaviors. It's appropriate

Figure 2.10: Jackie engages in conversation with a student.

Source: © 2017 by Plan Teach Assess. Used with permission.

Figure 2.11:
Balanced assessment combines products, performances, and conversations.

Source: © 2017 by Plan Teach Assess. Used with permission.

Gr. 3 - Reading Reflection

1. Sign into Halton Cloud

2. Go to shared with me, 2 finger tap, click add to my drive

3. Go to my drive, click your name -RR and click on reading response → make copy

4. Create reading response ✋

Figure 2.12:
Jackie's instructions informing students how to create reading responses.

Source: © 2016 by Jackie Clarke. Used with permission.

to continue to assess certain knowledge outcomes in traditional ways. For example, if students need to commit to memory a set of safety rules to ensure they engage in science lab work with minimum risk to life and limb, then a written quiz is a valid method to assess this learning. But memorizing such rules is no guarantee students will follow them in the heat of an experiment. So observing students actually behaving in safe ways in the science lab is essential.

Jackie utilizes a purposeful balance of products and observations to assess the reading skills of her third-grade students (see figure 2.11 and figure 2.12). She teaches her students to independently access their own reading performances from their cloud-based (online) storage accounts and compose their own reading responses (products) while she meets with individual students for brief, one-to-one conferences (conversations).

In Holly Moniz's seventh-grade class, students work in small groups to produce camera-ready infomercials (products) promoting the novels they have just read. (We first visited Holly in the Using Conversations and Performances for Formative Assessment section, page 22 in chapter 1.) However, throughout the formative stages of their work on the infomercials, she and the students observe their peers working together in groups. These observations serve as valuable feedback, enabling each group to revise the rough cut of the infomercial into a final product (see figure 2.13).

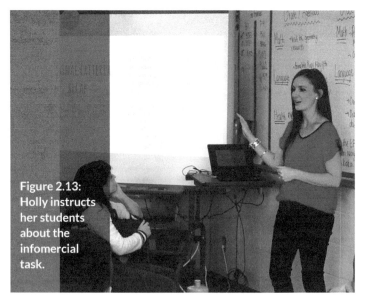

Figure 2.13: Holly instructs her students about the infomercial task.

Source: © 2017 by Plan Teach Assess. Used with permission.

Helen relies on a rich blend of performances, conversations, and products to assess her ninth-grade students' learning (see figure 2.14). Students each curate their own writing portfolio, which contains pieces reflecting every stage of the writing process, from initial ideas through to polished drafts (products). They also rehearse and present brief dramas based on texts they are reading (performances). But as you saw earlier in this chapter, Helen relies heavily on student conversation as an assessment strategy. With the novel seminar as the culminating summative assessment, she gradually builds students' skills and dispositions over the course of the entire semester so that, by the end of the course, they can demonstrate these learning outcomes with no teacher intervention.

In What Grades and Disciplines Should I Use Conversations and Performance-Based Observations?

Teachers of all grades and subjects must aim for an appropriately balanced assessment plan. What does that look like? Teachers should look to certain colleagues to see balanced assessment in action. Kindergarten and grades 1–2 teachers set the standard for assessing student

It's About Time

Jackie, Holly, and Helen all manage their time effectively and efficiently. They achieve this by beginning with the end in mind. That is to say, prior to beginning a unit of study, they use backward planning to identify essential learning outcomes. They develop summative assessments to determine whether all students have achieved these outcomes at the end of an instructional sequence, and then they plan differentiated instruction and formative assessment to respond to the different rates at which students move toward mastery.

**Figure 2.14:
Helen listens and observes as students conduct a novel seminar.**

Source: © 2017 by Plan Teach Assess. Used with permission.

learning through observation and conversation. Naturally, when students are too young to write, teachers must rely on their own skills as listeners and observers to track the growing competencies of their young charges. Unfortunately, these vital methods of assessment too often fall by the wayside once students can write. Look also to teachers of performance-based subjects—physical education, dance, and drama—to learn about assessment through observation at all grade levels.

Remember, much as we advocate for assessment through conversations and performances, written products continue to have their place. In particular, as long as postsecondary institutions continue to rely on term papers and formal examinations, high school teachers of college-track courses have a moral responsibility to prepare students to be successful on these often contrived and frequently invalid assessment methods. Generally speaking, once students can write, then written tasks are usually appropriate for assessing knowledge outcomes; for example, assessing knowledge of terms and procedures in science or factual content in social studies.

To assess simple skills, observe students as they perform. For example, if students have been taught how to focus and view slides using a microscope, then the most valid assessment strategy is to have students perform this task and describe what they see. To assess more complex competencies, as well as conceptual understanding, teachers should observe and converse with students as they engage in authentic performance tasks. If a teacher wishes to assess students' understanding of the numerous perspectives concerning climate change legislation, then having them assume the roles of the various agencies, businesses, and special interest groups involved in order to participate in a national or global forum will yield rich evidence of learning. Use figure 2.15 to assess your comfort level with using balanced assessment.

How to Plan Backward for Balanced Assessment

Change is difficult, messy, and rarely works the first time. So, altering your approach to assessment for balance by triangulating conversations, performances, and products requires careful planning and decision making. Collaboration among colleagues is sure to help ease this transition, and so we recommend taking the following steps.

1. Find at least one colleague with whom to work, learn, and problem solve.

2. Examine your current routines, and decide what you're going to *stop* doing to make time and energy available to implement a more balanced approach to assessment. In other words, identify the components of your assessment and grading practices you will replace with the gathering evidence of learning through observation and conversation.

3. Tell everyone who the changes will affect what you're planning to do. This means checking that your school's administrators are on board and supportive; informing parents about this initiative, and inviting their involvement; and of course, saying to your students, "We are going to try something new together."

The following sections further elaborate on backward-planning concepts, show them in action through a case study featuring Helen, and use that case study to explore why Helen made the choices she did and the benefits of her approach to backward planning.

Backward-Planning Concepts

We briefly introduced the concept of backward planning earlier in this chapter. Backward planning your approach to assessment is essential both to

Refer to your own curriculum, and identify standards and/or learning intentions you need to assess according to the following.

- Which can I best assess through conversation?
- Which can I best assess through observation?
- Which can I best assess through products?

Now take a moment to locate yourself on the following excerpt from the teacher-readiness scale. Select an appropriate task from the choices available.

	Curiosity *"I'm curious to learn about . . . ."*	**Commitment** *"I'm taking steps and beginning to . . . ."*	**Capacity** *"I'm building on my knowledge and skills for . . . ."*	**Confirmation** *"I'm proficient at, and helping others to . . . ."*
How do I assess learning using balanced assessment?	At least one simple way to gather evidence through observations and conversations	Gather evidence of learning through observations and conversations	Gathering evidence through observations and conversations	Gather, share, and involve students in assessing evidence through observations and conversations

Commitment-Level Application

Find a colleague with whom to plan and share your learning. Together, create either a performance task that you and your class will observe or a conversational assessment that you will record. Share with your colleague.

What went well? What did not? How might you both improve the task?

Capacity-Level Application

Working with a colleague, examine one subject area that you teach (elementary) or one course (secondary). Identify potential opportunities for replacing some of your traditional assessment strategies with assessment through observation of performance and through conversation. Develop a plan to gradually implement these new strategies.

Confirmation-Level Application

Convene a study group at your school to delve deeply into balanced assessment strategies with a goal of improving your collaborative practice.

Figure 2.15: Shift and Share—Balancing assessment.

*Visit **go.SolutionTree.com/assessment** for a free reproducible version of this figure.*

meet the needs of your students and to stay sane. When teachers begin their planning by identifying the essential learning that students must acquire by the end of a unit, term, or year, they have a clear focus to guide all their subsequent decisions. By next identifying what summative assessment tasks will be used to gather evidence of essential learning, they ensure that the connection between learning targets and corresponding assessments is airtight.

Teachers who start their planning with questions such as "What would be some fun activities to use during the first week of this unit?" inevitably find all the content they need to *cover* overwhelms them. And in the timeless words of researchers and authors Grant Wiggins and Jay McTighe (2005), *coverage* of learning by you, the teacher, is an inappropriate goal. Instead, teachers need to help students *uncover* their understanding through purposeful instruction and strategic assessment (Wiggins & McTighe, 2005). Planning with the end in mind is important for the following three reasons.

1. To ensure students master all essential learning

2. To ensure assessments provide evidence of that essential learning

3. To ensure the teacher differentiates instruction to enable all students to learn

These reasons necessitate a three-stage approach that not only ensures you provide balanced assessments but also that your instruction supports those assessments (Wiggins & McTighe, 2005).

1. **Identify essential learning:** This includes big ideas, essential understanding, and essential skills and competencies. It is the learning that must stick for students long after they move on from a given instructional unit.

2. **Design assessments to provide evidence of essential learning:** These comprise the set of assessment tasks, possibly organized in a portfolio, and including conversations, performances, and products that teachers will use to gather evidence of all the essential learning.

3. **Plan differentiated instruction:** This includes all lessons, inside and outside class experiences, as well as formative assessments that will identify gaps in learning to inform subsequent teaching.

Case Study: Helen Hills

Let's examine the backward-design process through a case study focusing on Helen's ninth-grade ELA class, whom we first visited in the Balanced Assessment and the VOCAL Approach section

(page 15 in chapter 1). Helen is an experienced teacher who passionately believes in the capacity of all students to learn. She knows all students can attain mastery of essential learning associated with her course if she implements the following.

- Clear expectations for students' coursework and behaviors

- Numerous opportunities to practice and get things wrong at first

- Procedures for ongoing and targeted oral and written feedback, along with the expectation that students will incorporate such feedback into their next efforts

- Variable pacing of instruction and assessment to suit the variety of students' needs

For this case study, let's focus on just an excerpted portion of Helen's ninth-grade ELA curriculum (see figure 2.16).

As part of her backward plan, Helen has decided that having groups of students participate in a novel seminar near the end of the course will enable her to summatively assess students' mastery of these learning outcomes. So her planning for this task involves working backward from the final performance of the novel seminar, breaking it down into the entire set of knowledge, skill, and behavioral components necessary to successfully engage in the seminar. Figure 2.17 identifies Helen's complete plan for this course, but our focus will be limited to how she planned backward from the novel-seminar oral performance.

In Helen's plan, you will see that there are three (triangulated) summative assessments, with each of these enabling her to gather evidence of some of the essential learning for the complete ninth-grade course. She plans formative and diagnostic assessments backward from these summative components to ensure that students are building necessary proficiency throughout the course in order to, ultimately, be successful on these and to assess levels of prior learning before beginning

Oral Communication (Overall Expectations)

1. **Listening to understand:** listen in order to understand and respond appropriately in a variety of situations for a variety of purposes

2. **Speaking to communicate:** use speaking skills and strategies appropriately to communicate with different audiences for a variety of purposes

Reading and Literature Studies (Overall Expectations)

1. **Reading for meaning:** read and demonstrate an understanding of a variety of literary, informational, and graphic texts, using a range of strategies to construct meaning

2. **Understanding form and style:** recognize a variety of text forms, text features, and stylistic elements, and demonstrate understanding of how they communicate meaning

Source for standards: Ontario Ministry of Education, 2007b.

Figure 2.16: Excerpts from Helen's ninth-grade ELA curriculum.

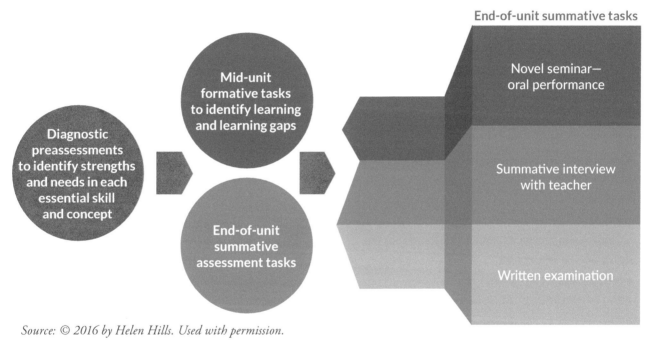

Source: © 2016 by Helen Hills. Used with permission.

Figure 2.17: An adapted version of Helen's assessment plan for her ninth-grade ELA course.

her instruction. In video 2.1, Helen describes her approach.

Watching this video, you can see that Helen has chosen to employ the novel seminar performance to serve the following purposes.

- Students must speak knowledgeably about the novel's theme, using specific references from the text to support their arguments.

- Students must make inferences from the text and make connections both within the text and with respect to their own experiences.

Video 2.1: Backward Design in Assessment Planning

Helen describes part of what her backward-planning process looks like.

Source: © 2017 by Plan Teach Assess. Used with permission.

- In terms of speaking and listening skills, students must articulate their ideas clearly, build on their peers' ideas, and challenge others respectfully when appropriate.

- Students must listen attentively, question the ideas of others, and provide encouragement, as necessary.

So, at the beginning of the course, Helen created simple, teacher-directed tasks that would provide instruction as well as formative feedback on the embedded skills and behaviors. Helen's goal is to always have her students progress to independence on each of these smaller tasks, knowing that the final summative novel seminar will require them to self-direct and self-monitor. This is a concept and framework educators often refer to as *gradual release of responsibility* (Fisher & Frey, 2014; Pearson & Gallagher, 1983).

A Question of *Why*

Through my interview with Helen, I wanted to explore why she chose to have students engage in these lengthy, self-directed novel seminars rather than using a more conventional assessment task such as a book report or an oral presentation. Here is a portion of that interview.

- **Does conversation differ from traditional assessment tasks?**

  You are going to hear more from them in an informal discussion. It may not be as well organized. It may not be as well supported. But if you listen to them, especially the boys, all of them had page references. All of them had very specific plot references. It was very evident that they knew the novel, so the knowledge portion was there. And then it was very obvious that they had all thought about very different types of connections and could explain those and articulate them. What I find is the huge difference between listening to students speak and having them write something. They still

get very nervous and struggle with structure at this stage and articulating their ideas through writing. But when they are allowed to speak, they are much more articulate. In terms of the formal presentations, this class did very well with that, and we do it really early on, but it's very limited, and it's highly structured, so they are a bit boring, to tell you the truth. With the spontaneous connections they make, I think it's much more interesting for them. They are more engaged, and it's much more interesting for me.

- **What are your assessment criteria?**

  I am looking for inferencing skills. I am looking for specific references to the text. I am looking for connections beyond the text. I am looking for their interpersonal speaking skills. So they're listening. So you would hear a kid start in when someone else was speaking, and they'd apologize and say, "You go ahead." Listening to what other people have to say and then be able to build on other responses or disagree in a polite manner. So it's the stylistic issues of speaking and listening as well as content and knowledge and then being able to analyze what they have read as well.

- **Will you use this evidence for formative or summative purposes?**

  It will be used for their grade, and it is for the oral component of the curriculum. The rubric was shared with the students before they started reading the novel, and then we talked more about the seminars. The students were given a sheet about what does a seminar look like, sound like, feel like, and they had to fill that out. They look at the rubric with all the teacher talk right from the [Ontario] Ministry of Education, and then they match up their saying, "What does it look, sound, feel like?" to the teacher talk. So they know how they are supposed to exhibit these skills in the seminar. And we will also tomorrow fill out a reflection sheet, sort of metacognition about how they did. And that will go in their portfolio, which we use later. (H. Hills, personal communication, November 7, 2016)

Benefits of Backward Planning

Let's now view the fruits of Helen's planning. In video 2.2, ninth-grade students working as a group have all read the novel *The Song of Kahunsha* by Canadian novelist Anosh Irani (2007). As these students engage in their discussion, Helen sits off to the side, using the rubric in figure 2.18 (page 52) to assess each student's demonstration of the required skills and behaviors. As the students speak, she looks for evidence of the success criteria.

Video 2.2: A Novel Seminar Student Conversation

A group of ninth-grade students discusses *The Song of Kahunsha* (Irani, 2007).

Source: © 2017 by Plan Teach Assess. Used with permission.

Note that in addition to the skills associated with reading and responding to a text, Helen is also able to assess students' collaboration skills using the list of learning skills. The chart in figure 2.19 (page 53) identifies the behavioral indicators she is looking for as the group members interact. Use her approach and the Shift and Share in figure 2.20 (page 53) to consider your own approach and level of readiness to engage in backward planning.

Key Messages

As you reflect on this chapter, we urge you to focus on the following key messages.

1. Balanced assessment, which means triangulating your approach to assessment, includes an appropriate blend of performance tasks, conversations, and products.

2. Triangulation of evidence also means ensuring you have at least three assessments on which to base summative judgments about student learning.

3. Assessment through observation and conversation is necessary at all grade levels and in all subject areas.

4. Planning for assessment should employ the principles of backward design; work from essential learning outcomes; match summative assessment tasks to these outcomes; design formative assessments and processes that scaffold students' learning; and tailor instruction to meet the needs of different groups of students.

Seminar

Learning Skills	Proficiency Level	Success Criteria
Responsibility	E G S N	Completes and submits work according to agreed-on timelines
Organization	E G S N	Identifies, gathers, evaluates, and uses information and resources to complete tasks
Independent work	E G S N	Uses class time appropriately to complete tasks
Initiative	E G S N	Demonstrates curiosity and interest in learning
Collaboration	E G S N	Works with others to resolve conflicts and build consensus to achieve group goals
Self-regulation	E G S N	Perseveres and makes an effort when responding to challenges

Assessment scale: E—Excellent; G—Good; S—Satisfactory; N—Needs Improvement

Seminar Knowledge and Skills

	Curriculum Criteria	Level 3	Seminar Criteria (To be created in class)	Evaluation
Application / Thinking / Knowledge — Conventions, style, and constructing meaning / Constructing meaning	Identify the important ideas and supporting details in your text. Demonstrate your knowledge and understanding of the key terms relevant to the topic. Make and explain *inferences* about your text. Support your explanations with well-chosen details and references from the text. *Analyze* your text in terms of the information, ideas, issues, or themes it explores, examining how various aspects of the text contribute to the presentation or development of these elements. Identify several different elements of style in texts and explain how they help communicate meaning and enhance the effectiveness of text. Extend your understanding of the text by making connections to the ideas in the text and your personal knowledge, experience, and insights; other texts; and the world around you. Refer to specific details in your text to explain your connections.	Demonstrates considerable understanding of the content Uses processing skills with considerable effectiveness Uses critical and creative thinking processes with considerable effectiveness Makes connections within and between various texts and ideas with considerable effectiveness Communicates with the intended audience with considerable effectiveness		

Assessment scale: Level 4—Exceeds standard; Level 3—Meets standard; Level 2—Approaching standard; Level 1—Below standard

Source: © 2016 by Helen Hills. Used with permission.

Figure 2.18: Helen's observation rubric for assessing the novel seminar.

*Visit **go.SolutionTree.com/assessment** for a free reproducible version of this figure.*

Learning Skills and Work Habits	Sample Behavioral Standards
Collaboration	The student: • Accepts various roles and an equitable share of work in the group • Responds positively to the ideas, opinions, values, and traditions of others • Builds healthy peer-to-peer relationships through personal and media-assisted interactions • Works with others to resolve conflicts and build consensus to achieve group goals • Shares information, resources, and expertise and promotes critical thinking to solve problems and make decisions

Source for standards: Ontario Ministry of Education, 2010.

Figure 2.19: Helen assesses using these behavior and communication skills during the novel seminar.

Take a moment to locate yourself on the following excerpt from the teacher-readiness scale, and then answer the questions that follow.

	Curiosity *"I'm curious to learn about . . . ."*	Commitment *"I'm taking steps and beginning to . . . ."*	Capacity *"I'm building on my knowledge and skills for . . . ."*	Confirmation *"I'm proficient at, and helping others to . . . ."*
How do I plan balanced assessment?	Developing assessment plans that include observations and conversations	Develop assessment plans that include evidence from observations and conversations	Developing assessment plans that reflect an appropriate balance of written, oral, and performance evidence	Design assessment plans that include a purposeful balance of written, oral, and performance evidence

How familiar are you with backward planning? Is this an area you need or wish to learn more about? If so, do some online research. If you have the time, locate and read *Understanding by Design* by Wiggins and McTighe (2005).

Select one unit and examine the assessment components for balance. Have you planned to gather evidence of learning through observation and conversation, as well as through student-written products?

Use the following questions to match your summative assessment tasks to essential learning outcomes.

• What enduring understandings and essential skills must all students acquire by the end of this unit or term?

• What summative assessment evidence must I gather to provide proof that students have mastered these essential learnings?

Figure 2.20: Shift and Share—Backward planning.

*Visit **go.SolutionTree.com/assessment** for a free reproducible version of this figure.*

How Do I Assess Learning Through Conversations and Performances?

Whenever students are demonstrating skills, teachers or their peers may engage in assessment through observation and conversation. Activities like solving a complex mathematics problem, collaborating with peers to gather data about their carbon footprint, or rehearsing a dramatic performance all involve both conversation as well as performance and therefore provide opportunities for teacher, peer, or self-assessment.

Since both conversations and performances demand the assessor's presence (either face-to-face or online) for the duration of the assessment, assessment through conversations and performances is time-consuming and requires strategic planning, both to ensure teachers can gather sufficient data and to prevent data overload (see figure 3.1).

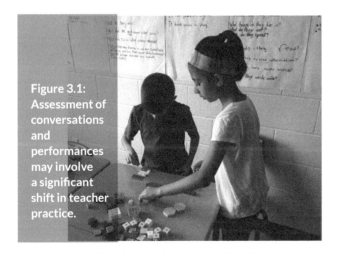

Figure 3.1: Assessment of conversations and performances may involve a significant shift in teacher practice.

Source: © 2017 by Plan Teach Assess. Used with permission.

In this chapter, we begin with common questions about assessment through observation and conversation, which include case studies from three teachers about how they set up classroom routines that facilitate and enable assessment through observation and conversation. With those examples

in mind, you'll explore the common features of classrooms with a strong culture of learning and how those features support the conversational and performance-based components of balanced assessment. We conclude with a look at who does the assessing.

Questions About Assessment Through Observation and Conversation

The following sections address common questions we hear from teachers about assessing through observation and conversation.

What Kinds of Conversations Should I Assess?

Meet Blake, a ninth grader. It's the end of September, and he is struggling in mathematics. He has just completed a quiz his teacher administered to assess students' understanding of place value, foundational knowledge for this grade level, which Blake should have acquired at a much earlier grade level. Blake failed the quiz. Jeff Catania, Blake's teacher, reacts to this by having a one-on-one conversation with Blake about the quiz (see video 3.1, page 56).

As you view the video, consider the following look-fors.

- Note how Jeff asks Blake to explain his thinking with probing questions without direct teaching.

Video 3.1: Diagnostic Interview and Intervention

Jeff talks with Blake to explore Blake's difficulties with foundational skills.

Source: © 2017 by Plan Teach Assess. Used with permission.

It's About Time

Clearly, this one-to-one conversation between teacher and student is an invaluable intervention when diagnosing the root cause of a lack of foundational skills for a class or grade level. "But how can I possibly find the time to have one-to-one conversations with all my students?" you ask. First, it is unlikely that a teacher would have to engage in such conversations with a large number of students. A quiz (such as the one Jeff uses) will identify the few students in the class demonstrating large deficits in learning. For these students, Jeff will need to have uninterrupted conversations like the one in video 3.1. This necessitates Jeff be proactive with lesson planning, ensuring the rest of the class has meaningful, engaging work to do.

- Notice that even when Blake's responses are correct, he lacks confidence and conviction. This highlights the fragility of his mathematical understanding. However, with Jeff's prompting, Blake is able to make remarkable progress in a short time, filling gaps in his understanding, which may have been in place for years.

- Watch for the degree of teacher neutrality in the conversation, which allows space for student confidence to emerge.

- Think about Jeff's tablet setup prior to the interview, which allows him to record this diagnostic interview for later review and to be more aware during the interaction to discern subtle instructional cues and learning moments.

- Notice how Jeff uses the conversation about Blake's quiz to not only diagnose Blake's confusion about place value but also to remediate it.

This is but one scenario in which assessment through conversation provides invaluable insight into a student's learning, in this case, into some fundamental gaps in Blake's prior knowledge about place value. What are some other scenarios? ELA teachers can glean rich background about students' reading habits and attitudes, including the home context, by having one-on-one conversations at the beginning of the academic year (diagnostic assessment). When engaged in scientific inquiry, having brief conversations with individual students enables the teacher to probe for understanding of the scientific process, including testing hypotheses, gathering data, identifying variables, and so on (formative assessment). When students have been involved in a summative role-play simulation (see the G7 simulation described in Assessing Skills and Competencies, page 40 in chapter 2), having a one-on-one conversation with each group member enables the teacher to check for individual understanding of concepts and individual contributions to the group's performance, as well as assess each student's capacity for self-reflection and metacognition (summative assessment). For students whose performance throughout the term has reflected a solid grasp of the learning, yet whose performance on a traditional test was uncharacteristically poor, a conversation provides teachers with the opportunity to probe student learning in a relatively stress-free way (summative assessment). Here are three other examples of assessment through conversation.

1. Conduct teacher-student conversations to set and monitor progress toward goals. (See the Case Study: Jackie Clarke section, page 111 in chapter 5, for a reading-improvement example.)

2. Facilitate student-student conversations to review acquired learning. (See the Case Study: Jamie Mitchell section in this chapter, page 58.)

3. Engage in conversations with small groups to reveal deep understanding of unit content. (See the Case Study: Helen Hills section in chapter 2, page 48.)

Ultimately, teachers must see their work to observe and converse with students and engage in differentiated instruction as necessary, not as a reactive, annoying add-on but as a planned and necessary aspect of every teacher's work (see figure 3.2).

Pause and Reflect

- Why does Jeff address Blake's misconceptions with guiding questions as opposed to procedural explanations?

- Are there elements of Jeff's approach that you could incorporate into your own practice?

- How can teachers find the time to engage in essential conversations with students who are having difficulties?

Figure 3.2: Conversing with and observing students require effective classroom routines.

How Do I Establish Classroom Routines That Facilitate Assessment Through Observation and Conversation?

Effective classroom routines are essential if teachers are to successfully implement a balanced approach to assessment. Regardless of the grade level, students must learn how to self-monitor and self-adjust their behaviors to enable teachers to meet with them individually or in small groups.

It is intentional that all the teachers featured in this book—teachers who have successfully implemented the VOCAL approach—are experts at establishing and monitoring effective classroom routines.

Source: © 2017 by Plan Teach Assess. Used with permission.

To achieve this goal, teachers must spend considerable time and effort, beginning on the first day of the term or year, establishing, monitoring, and maintaining a classroom culture that facilitates learning for all students. In the following sections, you'll see three examples of teachers who use a VOCAL approach to achieve student buy-in with behaviors that support a classroom culture where learning thrives, as does teachers' ability to assess learning through conversations and performances.

Case Study: Jamie Mitchell

Jamie Mitchell is a high school mathematics teacher and mathematics program leader at Dr. Frank J. Hayden Secondary School in Burlington, Ontario. He places great importance on the potential all students have to support and learn from each other.

As you will see in video 3.2, pairs of students engage in peer assessment to provide feedback to each other. They also rehearse responses, again to facilitate feedback, prior to having summative interviews with their teacher.

Video 3.2: Collaboration and Student Self-Monitoring

Jamie explains how he establishes classroom routines for his students.

Source: © 2017 by Plan Teach Assess. Used with permission.

After viewing video 3.2, consider how Jamie describes the routines he uses for his high school mathematics classes:

> We have been in groups like this since the beginning of the semester. It's how students arrive to class. It's what they are used to. Certainly, the first few weeks were an exercise in making sure that the students understood that while they were in groups, they needed to be working on math or talking about math. And while there are elevated conversation levels, most of the time when I circulate around, they are all talking about math in one way or another. And since they are used to working this way, I think, by and large, when I need to be out of the classroom monitoring kids or doing interviews, or I need to be at the other side of the classroom working with students who need a little more help, the other groups are definitely on task and doing what they need to be doing. . . . For the most part, they are self-monitoring. Twice a semester, I have them self-assess their learning skills to gauge where they are, and if I do notice behaviors happening that

are outside of the classroom norm, I address that. (Rebooting Assessment, 2021cc)

Case Study: Jackie Clarke

For this case study (see video 3.3), listen to Jackie Clarke describe how her own understanding of *locus of control* (Kutanis & Mesci, 2011; Nowicki & Strickland, 1973) informs her approach to routines in her third-grade classroom.

Video 3.3: Building a Cooperative Environment

Jackie describes her own understanding of locus of control and how it informs her approach to classroom routines.

Source: © 2017 by Plan Teach Assess. Used with permission.

There are three key concepts Jackie addresses in video 3.3 in response to a question about how teachers influence student behaviors:

> What is it about the kids that is causing the behavior? Why do kids do what they do, and how are we setting them up to be successful? I started realizing that when you have engaging tasks, when you have a classroom built on community, you don't have behavior problems. I even reflected back to my own learning, sitting in rows or sitting in groups of two, and the quietest kids did the best because they didn't bother the teacher because they sat at their desks. So that was actually one of the environmental things in my classroom that I got rid of, which was having the teacher's desk because to me that is a power thing. (Rebooting Assessment, 2021aa)

Key to Jackie effectively working one-to-one with students is the work she does beforehand with the whole class to establish classroom routines. From the first day of school in September, Jackie works with her students to help them understand the importance of a set of learning skills that will enable them to work together throughout the year in a respectful, collaborative, and productive manner:

> I took out the word **rules** in my classroom because I think rules are meant to be broken. Kids, if they have belief statements and they believe something, they follow through. So that is why we call them our **beliefs**. . . .The other thing I have always looked at is engaging, meaningful, authentic tasks. When kids are pumped, come through the door, they can't wait. . . .I had kids today who didn't want to leave making symmetry. I couldn't get them to go to music fast enough because they didn't want to stop. (Rebooting Assessment, 2021aa)

The district where Jackie works assesses students at all grade levels using an established set of generic behavioral expectations set by the Ontario Ministry of Education (see figure 3.3, page 60).

Although Jackie must assess students based on these behavioral expectations, instead of simply presenting them to her young charges as *fait accompli*, Jackie takes the time to cocreate an anchor chart for each set of skills with her students, using student-friendly language. She does this work one set of skills at a time, according to when a given skill set first arises. For example, when she first introduces her yearlong process for improving each student's reading skills, she talks about the importance of the rest of the class being able to work independently. However, because Jackie is highly skilled at allowing students to work in different ways at the same time, she acknowledges the need to also develop an anchor chart for collaboration. Figure 3.4 (page 61) shows the two anchor charts that emerged as a result of her work with students to identify behavioral indicators for independence and collaboration.

Learning Skills and Work Habits

E–Excellent G–Good S–Satisfactory N–Needs Improvement

Responsibility ☐

- Fulfills responsibilities and commitments in the learning environment
- Completes and submits classwork, homework, and assignments according to agreed-on timelines
- Takes responsibility for and manages own behavior

Organization ☐

- Devises and follows a plan and process for completing work and tasks
- Establishes priorities and manages time to complete tasks and achieve goals
- Identifies, gathers, evaluates, and uses information, technology, and resources to complete tasks

Independent Work ☐

- Independently monitors, assesses, and revises plans to complete tasks and meet goals
- Uses class time appropriately to complete tasks
- Follows instructions with minimal supervision

Collaboration ☐

- Accepts various roles and an equitable share of work in a group
- Responds positively to the ideas, opinions, values, and traditions of others
- Builds healthy peer-to-peer relationships through personal and media-assisted interactions
- Works with others to resolve conflicts and build consensus to achieve group goals
- Shares information, resources, and expertise, and promotes critical thinking to solve problems and make decisions

Initiative ☐

- Looks for and acts on new ideas and opportunities for learning
- Demonstrates the capacity for innovation and a willingness to take risks
- Demonstrates curiosity and interest in learning
- Approaches new tasks with a positive attitude
- Recognizes and advocates appropriately for the rights of self and others

Self-Regulation ☐

- Sets own individual goals and monitors progress toward achieving them
- Seeks clarification or assistance when needed
- Assesses and reflects critically on own strengths, needs, and interests
- Identifies learning opportunities, choices, and strategies to meet personal needs and achieve goals
- Perseveres and makes an effort when responding to challenges

Source for standards: Ontario Ministry of Education, 2010.

Figure 3.3: Evaluation form for student behavioral skills.

By the end of September, Jackie and her students have cocreated anchor charts for all six skill areas the district designates (see figure 3.5). Each time one of the skill clusters is going to be important for student learning, Jackie takes the time to review it before setting the class to work. Just as important, once the task is complete, she and her students assess their success with respect to both the academic learning intentions and the learning skills (see figure 3.6).

Conversation characterizes Jackie's interaction with her students, whether in a whole-class setting or when working with individuals, but not the typical question-and-answer approach common to traditionally organized classrooms. For example, the

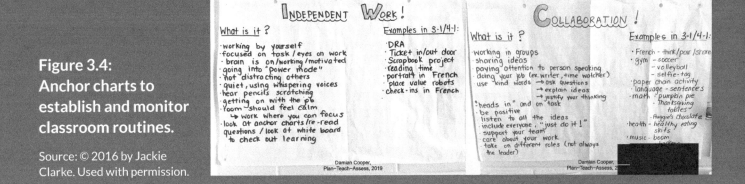

Figure 3.4: Anchor charts to establish and monitor classroom routines.

Source: © 2016 by Jackie Clarke. Used with permission.

Figure 3.5: A complete set of anchor charts that students reference as they collaborate around related skills.

Source: © 2016 by Jackie Clarke; © 2017 by Plan Teach Assess. Used with permission.

Figure 3.6: Jackie schedules time for conversations with students, who all remain productive during interview time.

Source: © 2016 by Jackie Clarke; © 2017 by Plan Teach Assess. Used with permission.

It's About Time

When I asked Jackie, "How can you afford the time to collaborate with the children to create anchor charts for each of these learning skills?", she replied:

That's a great question and one I hear from many of my colleagues. I always respond by saying that anything that is new will take time. It's a learning curve for everyone, just like when we teach a new concept to our students. However, when we realize the long-term positive impact for our students, their families, and ourselves as educators, the time investment upfront is absolutely worth it (J. Clarke, personal communication, October 30, 2016).

anchor charts for the six behavioral skills derive from rich, teacher-guided conversations that follow either a role-play activity in the classroom or the viewing of a short video that clearly demonstrates one of the learning skills.

Case Study: Helen Hills

As a further example, consider how Helen Hills, whom you met in chapter 2 (page 34), teaches her ninth-grade students to behave and interact appropriately, regardless of whether they are in a group directly engaged in the novel seminar task or are left unsupervised in the classroom while she assesses each seminar group (see figure 3.7).

Given that Helen conducts each of the novel seminars sitting in a hallway of the school, the obvious question is, "What is the rest of the class doing?" In this case, Helen began the class by explaining that two novel seminars would occur during each seventy-minute class period. The participating group would meet in the hallway with her while the rest of the class worked on assigned tasks. Given this setup, Helen must be able to count on the rest of her class self-monitoring and taking responsibility for the work she has set for them so that she can spend the time required to observe the seminars—in this case, a minimum of twenty minutes for each seminar. Yes, Helen left her ninth-grade class for more than forty minutes, confident that they would use the time wisely. Helen believes students can do whatever they are purposefully taught and supported to do, and her students don't disappoint her (see video 3.4).

Figure 3.7: Students engage in a recorded novel seminar discussion.

Source: © 2017 by Plan Teach Assess. Used with permission.

Source: © 2017 by Plan Teach Assess. Used with permission.

In particular, note how Helen connects a culture of respect in the classroom to learning:

> Then the learning becomes a lot easier for them, being able to voice their opinion without feeling like they are going to be judged or that somebody might laugh at them or correct them. So they feel confident speaking because they all have good ideas. They've done some formal presentations where they had to stand up in front of the class and speak, and the idea of respect is always an emphasis in my classroom. (Rebooting Assessment, 2021bb)

When I asked Helen what it took to get all her students to this level of responsibility, she replied, "The journey begins in September and is aimed, first and foremost, at developing respect in all of my students: respect for themselves, respect for their teacher, and respect for their classmates" (H. Hills, personal communication, June 7, 2016). Despite these being adolescent students, I observed first-hand that their behavior was exemplary, and it was clear to me as an outside observer that Helen is a true expert in terms of setting and monitoring behavioral expectations for her students. During my interview with Helen, she said:

> They are grade 9s. I don't expect them to be perfect. At the beginning of the semester, many of them frequently acted out. But by quietly drawing

attention to inappropriate behaviors and expecting students to take responsibility themselves for changing these behaviors, they all come round. (H. Hills, personal communication, June 7, 2016)

This comes across clearly in video 3.5, in which Helen describes her experience with a student acting contrary to behavioral expectations.

Source: © 2017 by Plan Teach Assess. Used with permission.

As Helen's comments indicate, she understands that adolescents are going to misbehave. But instead of reacting, she cuts them some slack. Let's look closer at what she says:

> I really do believe that all kids want to succeed, and they want to do well. They want to please. To give them that opportunity and to know that I am going to listen to each one of them and respect each one of them is really important. So when a kid does get silly—like yesterday, a kid threw a bag of chips across the room. He was just being excited. He was just being a fourteen-year-old. He said, "I just wanted to give you the chips." He was trying to give me a bag of chips, but he threw them at me! I'm not going to yell at him. I called him over, and we talked about the fact that you don't throw a bag of chips at your teacher. So it's an ongoing process. (Rebooting Assessment, 2021bb)

Helen deeply understands the need to model the same required skills and behaviors she and the school district expect of students. She then provides opportunities for her students to practice these skills and behaviors while receiving feedback from her and gradually releases the responsibility for self-monitoring and self-correcting to students.

Following the complete twenty-minute seminar, I remarked to Helen how astounded I was at the composure and maturity of the boys. Helen said, "That's what grade 9 boys can do if you get out of the way!" (H. Hills, personal communication, June 7, 2016).

Who Does the Assessing?

Teachers don't have the time to be the only person in the room responsible for assessment. Furthermore, when teachers require students themselves to examine their own work and the work of their peers, they engage in truly critical thinking. But to be clear, I am not advocating students evaluating or grading their own or each other's work. That is exclusively the teacher's responsibility.

Self- and peer assessment both involve students examining, with a critical eye, performances, conversations, and products, relative to a clear set of criteria. These criteria may be reflected in a checklist, a rubric, a set of anchor pieces, or a combination of these tools. In its exemplary form, self- and peer assessment involve a student critically examining his or her own or a peer's work, followed by the student conveying orally, in writing, or in combination,

his or her reflections on the work in terms of its strengths, weaknesses, and most important, what changes to content or approach would lead to improvement (see figure 3.8). Note that this "work" doesn't have to be a tangible product; it could just as easily be in a VOCAL context—a demonstration of skills, a conversation, or a performance.

Figure 3.8: Seventh-grade students engage in peer assessment of formative work.

Source: © 2017 by Plan Teach Assess. Used with permission.

Even in early childhood, students are capable of metacognition (Cohen, Opatosky, Savage, Stevens, & Darrah, 2021). Thus, teachers should expect students at any grade level, beginning in kindergarten, to engage in the metacognitive process of self- and peer assessment (provided the assessment purpose is formative). But, as we state at the start of this section, when the purpose of the assessment is summative (occurs at the end of a unit, term, or year) and it involves grading, then the teacher *must* be the arbiter of quality. I like to don my parent hat in this regard and categorically say, "No part of my child's grade must be determined by or influenced by what another child has done."

On the other hand, students and their peers can gather a great deal of the formative evidence of their learning. The research concerning assessment *for* and *as* learning is compelling (Black & Wiliam, 1998; Earl, 2013; Wiliam, 2018). Students must be directly involved in the assessment process to understand how to improve their own work. So, the teacher's ultimate goal is to have each student become a reliable, autonomous monitor and adjuster of his or her own performance. As long as students are dependent on the teacher to tell them what they need to do differently to improve their work or behavior, they haven't truly learned.

The following sections address student roles specific to self-assessment and peer assessment.

Self-Assessment

Recall from chapter 1 (page 12), *formative assessment* in the control of the teacher is often called assessment *for* learning. When students are in control of their own assessment, then educators use the term assessment *as* learning (Earl, 2013). Assessment *as* learning is powerful because it requires students to reflect on their own performance and decide what they are doing well, where problems exist, and what they need to do differently to improve. This process of self-monitoring and self-adjusting performance (*metacognition*, or thinking about one's own thinking) is a critical skill that teachers can help students develop (Cohen et al., 2021).

Teachers who gradually but intentionally shift control over formative assessment from themselves to their students understand that the gradual release of responsibility to students, a concept we introduced earlier in this chapter, is essential to developing autonomy and independence. For example, Jackie empowers her third-grade students to become highly effective assessors of their own work. In her individualized reading program, she uses a powerful blend of teacher, self-, and peer assessment to set, monitor, and achieve the improvement goals she establishes for students at key points during the school year. Video 3.6, video 3.7, and video 3.8 illustrate Jackie's approach.

By taking the time to train her students in the skills of self- and peer assessment, Jackie can devote significant time to individualized instruction, confident that the rest of the class is meaningfully engaged. (See chapter 5, page 104, for a complete case study of Jackie's application of the VOCAL approach to learning.)

Peer Assessment

Jamie regularly shares the responsibility for assessment with his students by having them engage in peer assessment, but he first takes the necessary time to

Video 3.6: Teacher-Student Reading Conference

Jackie reviews reading goals with a student.

Source: © 2017 by Plan Teach Assess. Used with permission.

Video 3.7: Student Reviews Her Performance

A student watches a recording of her own reading performance to formatively self-assess.

Source: © 2017 by Plan Teach Assess. Used with permission.

Video 3.8: Student Reflects on Her Performance

A student makes notes about what she has to work on to improve her reading skills.

Source: © 2017 by Plan Teach Assess. Used with permission.

Video 3.9: Teacher Gives Instruction for Peer Assessment

Jamie explains to his students how they will rehearse for a peer-assessment activity.

Source: © 2017 by Plan Teach Assess. Used with permission.

Video 3.10: Two Students Engage in Peer Assessment

Two students engage in peer assessment as they prepare to demonstrate their learning at the end of a unit.

Source: © 2017 by Plan Teach Assess. Used with permission.

teach students how to self- and peer assess effectively. See an example in video 3.9. In video 3.10, you see his students put Jamie's guidance to work as they engage in peer assessment.

Elements of a Culture of Learning

All classrooms we visited during our research for this book, from kindergarten to grade 12, shared a number of common attributes. So, reflecting on the examples in the previous section, let's consider the elements of a culture of learning that we observed during our research. The following sections explore these elements in detail.

Teacher-Student Relationships Are Positive and Focused on Learning

Underpinning successful teaching and learning is the relationship between teachers and students. The following values characterized the classrooms we visited while conducting research for this book.

- **Respect:** For self, teachers, and peers
- **Collaboration:** According to agreed-on classroom norms
- **Optimism:** *Fail* means a *first attempt at learning*, with a mindset of, "I can do this!"
- **Encouragement:** Honest, sensitive feedback from teachers and peers

The teachers we observed modeled respect for themselves and their students in everything they said and did. Jamie treats his high school students as the young adults they are, trusting them to remain on task and to complete work responsibly, even when he is not supervising them directly. Jackie places great importance on collaboratively establishing norms—what she calls *beliefs*—for classroom behavior with her students, and she holds herself and students accountable, on a daily basis, for observing these. Holly Moniz has her intermediate-grade students spend a great deal of instructional time working in cooperative groups of four, confident they will self-monitor and support one another to accomplish their own learning goals (see figure 3.9). You'll see more of her practice in case studies in chapter 4 (page 74) and chapter 5 (page 104). Each of these teachers maintains a spirit of optimistic achievement in their classrooms so their students believe in themselves—what psychologist Albert Bandura (1994) and assessment expert Rick Stiggins (2009, 2020) call *self-efficacy*.

Teacher Directions Are Clear and Consistent

All the teachers we worked with demonstrated a high degree of efficiency regarding initiating classroom work. They gain the attention of all students before issuing instructions, provide both visual and oral cues about daily routines, check for understanding before setting students to work, ensure there are sufficient follow-up tasks for students who complete assigned work, and assess the success of the work period once it ends—and they use these strategies every day to exemplary effect.

Students Are Free to Move Around and Spend Time Talking

While there are times when it is necessary for students to be quietly seated at their desks, we believe these times should be the exception rather than the rule. Too often, especially in elementary classrooms, the most prevalent sound is the teacher saying, "Shhh." Young learners, like all human beings, are social creatures. Particularly during the early childhood years, social interaction helps children develop a variety of essential skills connected to working memory, executive-functioning skills, and cognitive flexibility (Kerr, Heller, Hulen, & Butler, 2021). The challenge for teachers is to establish clear behavioral expectations so that talk, movement, and action focus on learning and not individual students' distractions (see figure 3.10, page 68).

While the approach to instruction must change as students progress to later grades, students' need for interaction as part of the learning experience does not. Education leadership and instructional coaching expert Jane A. G. Kise (2021) asserts that many students

**Figure 3.9:
A culture of learning has multiple learning areas and rich resources.**

Source: © 2017 by Plan Teach Assess. Used with permission.

Figure 3.10: Highly engaging learning tasks.

Source: © 2017 by Plan Teach Assess. Used with permission.

It's About Time

Although we often hear teachers lament that they don't have enough time for all they must do, we also find that inefficient use of instructional time is common in many classrooms. In particular, inefficient strategies for taking attendance, and frequent interruptions from students arriving late, characterize the first and last minutes of lessons and time blocks. From public address (PA) system announcements to attention-seeking behaviors from students, a wide variety of interruptions characterizes many of the classrooms we have visited over the years. By contrast, the teachers involved in this project all took proactive steps to minimize interruptions and maximize instructional time. These included establishing clear daily routines, clarifying their daily expectations of students, using a blend of instructional strategies that included social interaction, and undertaking daily reflection on and assessment of the day's lesson.

(and adults) have a very strong cognitive preference for experience and movement when engaging in learning tasks and that long chunks of direct instruction or individual study make it difficult for these students to maintain a focus on learning. Therefore, learning activities that get such students moving while promoting interaction with peers and physical learning materials help sustain their focus.

Time on Task Is Maximized With Students Engaged in Meaningful Work

When students find assigned tasks engaging and have a sense that work is worthy of their time, they are more likely to invest energy and effort and to persevere when encountering challenges. While this is true at all grade levels, teachers in the middle and senior grades need to pay particular attention to the quality of work they require students to complete. The least effective way to promote student commitment is to attach marks and grades as motivators since they merely foster students' desire for extrinsic rewards. Teachers are better advised to assign work that is intrinsically rewarding. In other words, students seek to be successful because the work is in and of itself rewarding. Think of the novel seminar Helen Hills conducted with her students earlier in this chapter (page 62).

Teachers Are Constantly Engaged With Students

Regardless of the grade level or subject, whole-class instruction is often appropriate to review the previous day's work, introduce new learning, and check for understanding at the end of a lesson (Kise, 2021). But the critical midsection of a lesson, when students are engaging with new learning, requires teachers to constantly move around the room, interacting with individual students and student groups. Whether to clarify the demands of the task, uncover difficulties, cue prior knowledge, or encourage (see figure 3.11), when students are actively engaged in learning, the teacher should act as a coach and learning facilitator.

Consistent with this approach, we had difficulty locating those master teachers when we first entered their learning space; they remained active, engaging with and observing students throughout the school day. This is a good thing! It means one or more students were receiving guidance to support them in independent or group learning at all times.

Teachers Optimize Use of Space and Furniture

In classrooms with an effective culture of learning, teachers optimize available space for maximum productivity. The classrooms featured in our research all had multiple learning areas, moveable furniture, student access to meaningful resources, and prominently displayed work samples, as well as homey touches such as lamps and rugs (see figure 3.12 and figure 3.13, page 70). In many cases, teachers and students used spaces outside the classroom, such as the hallway, as an extension of the classroom to provide separation, privacy, or quiet as required.

By ensuring spaces to support both independent and group learning, teachers like those featured in this chapter support collaboration among peers and teacher-to-student guidance with numerous opportunities for movement, talk, passion, engagement, struggle, perseverance, reflection, and deep thinking (see figure 3.14, page 70). These learning environments make students feel safe engaging in productive struggle by asking questions,

**Figure 3.11:
A culture of learning—Visual cues for classroom norms.**

Source: © 2016 by Jackie Clarke. Used with permission.

Figure 3.12: A culture of learning—Visible artifacts, moveable furniture.

Source: © 2017 by Plan Teach Assess. Used with permission.

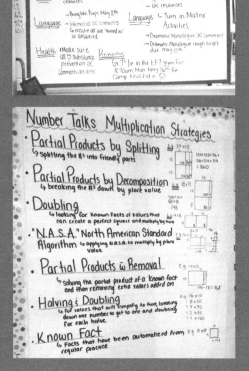

**Figure 3.13:
A culture of learning—Clear classroom routines.**

Source: © 2016 by Jackie Clarke. Used with permission.

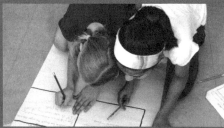

Figure 3.14: A culture of learning—Talking, engaging, questioning, reflecting, deep thinking, collaborating.

Source: © 2017 by Plan Teach Assess. Used with permission.

making mistakes, and trying again in response to feedback (Blackburn, 2018; Grafwallner, 2021). Use figure 3.15 to consider your approach to establishing and maintaining a culture of learning in your classroom and what next steps you might take to make your classroom even more welcoming to active learning experiences where observation and conversation support your assessment efforts. Then use figure 3.16 (page 72) to reflect on the different video segments throughout this chapter to evaluate your current position on the teacher-readiness scale and to determine next actions.

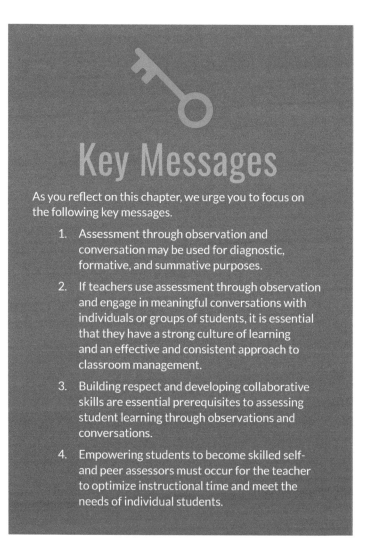

Key Messages

As you reflect on this chapter, we urge you to focus on the following key messages.

1. Assessment through observation and conversation may be used for diagnostic, formative, and summative purposes.

2. If teachers use assessment through observation and engage in meaningful conversations with individuals or groups of students, it is essential that they have a strong culture of learning and an effective and consistent approach to classroom management.

3. Building respect and developing collaborative skills are essential prerequisites to assessing student learning through observations and conversations.

4. Empowering students to become skilled self- and peer assessors must occur for the teacher to optimize instructional time and meet the needs of individual students.

Use the following list to help you identify changes you can make to optimize a culture of learning for you and your students.

Feature	Actions I Plan to Take
Does my classroom feature multiple learning areas?	
Are routines visible to students (for example, posted in the classroom)?	
Do I use cues (for example, verbal reminders to students) and routines effectively?	
Does learning involve students' peers as often as me?	
Are students free to move around to further their learning?	
Do I encourage students to talk?	
Do students view struggle as essential to learning?	
Do students feel safe making mistakes in order to learn?	
Does my teaching encourage perseverance, reflection, and deep thinking?	
Have I arranged the furniture to facilitate conversation?	

Figure 3.15: Shift and Share—A culture of learning.

*Visit **go.SolutionTree.com/assessment** for a free reproducible version of this figure.*

After reading chapter 3 and watching the video clips, take stock of your comfort level by reviewing the following two components on the teacher-readiness scale. Then, choose one of the tasks following the scale as a next step for your practice.

	Curiosity *"I'm curious to learn about . . . ."*	**Commitment** *"I'm taking steps and beginning to . . . ."*	**Capacity** *"I'm building on my knowledge and skills for . . . ."*	**Confirmation** *"I'm proficient at, and helping others to . . . ."*
How do I assess learning using balanced assessment?	At least one simple way to gather evidence through observations and conversations	Gather evidence of learning through observations and conversations	Gathering evidence through observations and conversations	Gather, share, and involve students in assessing evidence through observations and conversations
How do I use digital technology to implement balanced assessment?	How to watch and assess student performances or interviews live without technology	Allow students to use technology to capture evidence of their learning	Using cloud technology to capture, share, and manage evidence of students' learning	Use technology in a variety of ways to capture evidence of students' learning

Commitment-Level Application

Working with a colleague, plan and implement a formative assessment conversation strategy, similar to the Jeff and Blake example from this section. Share with your colleague what went well, what did not, and how you might both improve the task.

Capacity-Level Application

Locate one or more colleagues who are interested in using technology to support classroom assessment. Form a study group, and devise a plan to learn about and try using this approach for a term. (See chapter 4, page 74, for further guidance about supporting assessment using technology.)

Confirmation-Level Application

Convene a study group to conduct a research project into the culture of learning at your school. Use the "Shift and Share—A Culture of Learning" list (page 71) to gather data.

Figure 3.16: Shift and Share—Exploring balanced assessment.

*Visit **go.SolutionTree.com/assessment** for a free reproducible version of this figure.*

How Can I Use Technology to Support Assessment?

by Jeff Catania

Essential learning for students has evolved far beyond mere knowledge retention (memorization). Learning in a highly connected world requires a broad range of higher-order cognitive, social, and emotional competencies for life in school and beyond (Niemi, 2020; Partnership for 21st Century Learning, 2019). We explore these competencies in more detail in this chapter, but they include applying learning in different contexts, the capacity to listen to and build on others' ideas, critical thinking, emotional intelligence, and metacognition. Traditional tests and written assignments are generally less effective than conversations and performances for assessing these higher-order competencies, which illuminates the need for the VOCAL approach to reveal and nurture them in students.

Technology is pervasive in the VOCAL approach because of the way it enhances and enables assessment. The *see it, hear it, save it, assess it,* and *share it* components in our VOCAL graphic reflect how athletes, musicians, tradespeople, and gamers get inspired, learn new skills, and improve performance through direct observation using a variety of media. On the conversation side, chapters 1–3 clarified the central role dialogue and oral communication have in human life and learning and how essential that role is to balanced assessment practices at all grades and subject areas. Incorporating technology boosts these VOCAL approaches and provides relevance and engagement.

Source: © 2017 by Plan Teach Assess. Used with permission.

In this chapter, we explore four key benefits of using technology to support assessment and suggest a *ready, fire, aim* approach for technology adoption. From this foundation, we highlight three graduated ways to use information technology (IT) in your classroom and then explore some common technology challenges teachers may encounter. The chapter concludes with key messages you should take away from this chapter.

Four Key Benefits of Using Technology to Support Assessment

For some teachers, adopting technology brings some trepidation, while others feel thrilled to expand technology use broadly. Support for the former group, and guidance for the latter, on how to best employ the technology available to them will not just save time and improve assessment but has the potential to reboot the following.

- How teachers communicate (with colleagues, students, parents, and others)
- The depth and quality of learning materials students can access
- How teachers collect, analyze, and act on data about students' learning

The following sections focus on four key benefits to teachers of using technology to support balanced assessment: (1) seeing deeply into students' thinking, (2) promoting self- and peer assessment, (3) maximizing time for assessment, and (4) preserving evidence of learning.

Seeing Deeply Into Students' Thinking

I've taught many different high school subject areas (including physics, mathematics, communication technology, business, technical design, and computer studies), and though I used performances fairly regularly, I could count on one hand the number of times a conversation was assessed. Generally, I felt very comfortable having students write things on paper and then marking that paper.

Like me, some educators may focus on traditional ideas of learning and assessment through simple comfort, while others may consider observation and conversation as being too subjective. However, the first three chapters showed the use of recording technology in support of conversational and performance-based assessment is authentic, valid, reliable, and differentiated. Teachers and students have the option of recording, pausing, and rewatching performances or discussions, providing depth and insight into learning not always possible during a live interaction.

All this means that when teachers use technology to capture students engaging in conversation and performing learning tasks, they *see into* students thinking in ways the physical products of their work (worksheets, written assessments, and so on) cannot reveal. A myriad of deep, high-order student competencies become visible for feedback and improvement. These include the following.

- **Depth of understanding**: For students who struggle with written communication, gauging understanding through a video-recorded conversation will be more authentic and reliable. In a live interview or recorded performance, where there are prompts and redirections throughout, a more complete map of the nuances and branches of student understanding reveals itself.

- **Preconceptions, partial conceptions, and misconceptions:** These items can be challenging to discern in a written answer,

but they can be made available in dialogue, simultaneously making the assessment experience a learning experience.

- **Degree of tolerance for others' perspectives and capacity to listen and build on others' ideas:** Media capture of students interacting provides a unique opportunity to see into student thinking about other ideas and perspectives.

- **Use of learning strategies and metacognitive skills:** Interviews, performances, and dialogues all provide opportunities for practicing learning strategies such as making connections or having students reflect on their own thinking in the moment (rather than returning a quiz a week later).

Promoting Self- and Peer Assessment

Not only does recording conversations and performances provide rich evidence of learning, it also empowers students to review and assess their own performances, leading to improvement in learning (formative assessment) rather than just receiving a score. Cycles of self-feedback that lead to greater success create a positive feedback loop that increases student motivation to engage in more and more feedback. Ultimately, students move toward self-actualizing as their own best assessors.

Maximizing Time for Assessment

For most teachers, *time* is their most precious commodity (see figure 4.1). There may be resistance to learning new approaches (even time-saving ones) simply to avoid taking the time required to learn. Meanwhile, familiar, teacher-centric approaches (such as creating and marking a test) *feel* fast but actually take significant time over another approach (watching short, student-captured video of class groups interacting around a topic, for example).

With that in mind, table 4.1 illustrates how shifting from traditional approaches to learning and assessment toward VOCAL approaches achieves balanced assessment and saves time, especially with the support of technology.

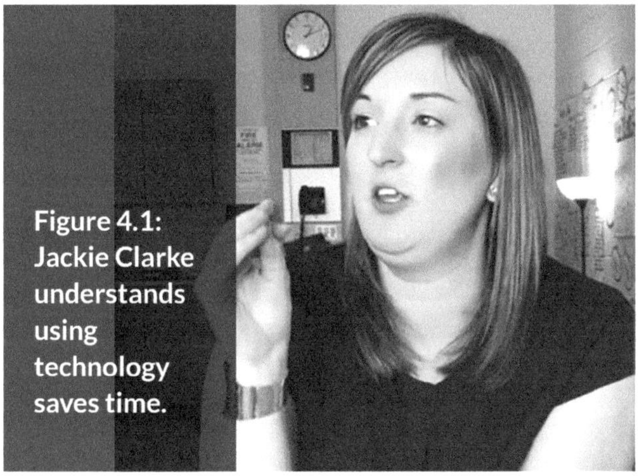

Figure 4.1: Jackie Clarke understands using technology saves time.

Source: © 2017 by Plan Teach Assess. Used with permission.

Using technology with a balance of communication and observation assessment practices allows teachers to do *more* and do it *more meaningfully*, with potentially even less time invested.

Preserving Evidence of Learning

One myth about the use of conversation and performance assessment is that the resulting assessments lack accountability without the typical paper trail traditional assessments produce. With the incorporation of technology, digital evidence of performance and conversation is now available easily and flexibly to support assessment decisions. In addition, stored evidence allows for many other advantages (see table 4.1) and opens up the possibility for multiple assessors

Table 4.1: How Technology and a VOCAL Approach Recapture Time

Traditional Approaches	The VOCAL Shift	It's About Time
More evidence is better	Balanced is better	When adding more conversation and observation in assessment, teachers then decide what product-based assessment they will cease.
Write (products)	Write (products), say (conversations), do (performances)	Conducting a short interview or observing a student doing a task for a few minutes may reveal more than any test could, and interviews can focus on students' individual areas of need, avoiding the gathering and marking of unnecessary evidence. Written work can still have a place to assess knowledge and basic skills quickly, in balance with other approaches.
Assess later	Assess now . . . or later	Live assessment (such as conducting a student interview while assessing on the fly) means nothing to take home and mark. Because in-class time is limited, capturing observational assessments also provides the option to review performances or conversations outside of class, similar to traditional written assessments.
Teacher focused	Student focused	Technology capture enables students to be more involved in their own evidence gathering, reviewing, and self-assessing, freeing up even more teacher and class time for deeper learning topics and tasks or to review areas highlighted in the recordings. As students develop more capacity, they can engage in increasingly deeper self-assessment, create their own success criteria, capture their own best learning, share it with others, and so on, saving even more time.
Push	Pull	Keeping digital, recorded evidence of student achievement means students, parents, and others can potentially self-serve (pull) evidence of learning at any time, rather than teachers having to take time sending, writing, and sharing reports to manually (push) evidence of learning.

Pause and Reflect

- If you use significant amounts of observation or conversation in your assessment practice, what got you started? If you haven't yet, what is holding you back?

- How much does technology intersect (or not) with your assessment practices?

- If you use technology with students, is it primarily in the context of conversations, performances, products, or a balance of all three?

(student, peer, teacher) to review and provide feedback, even at different times and places.

In short, gathering, analyzing, and sharing digital evidence of observations and conversations is not just the future of educational assessment, it is essential now (Palao, Hastie, Cruz, & Ortega, 2015; Reid et al., 2015; Tailab & Marsh, 2019). Damian sums it up when he says that in his forty years as an educator, he hasn't seen another innovation that holds greater promise for improving the learning of all students.

The *Ready, Fire, Aim* Approach to Technology Adoption

Some teachers aim to fully understand topics completely before standing in front of their students. However, it is that fear of things going wrong, or of appearing incompetent, that actually inhibits technology adoption more than any lack of understanding. Michael Fullan (2011), the highly respected Canadian researcher and thinker, recommends a *ready, fire, aim* mindset for implementing technology-supported changes as a way to overcome both the fear and inertia that can inhibit educators. Consider the following approaches to technology adoption to see where your own style fits in.

- **Ready, aim, fire:** This common approach starts with getting *ready* (learning the technology as a teacher in some way prior to using it with students), *aiming* (planning a careful lesson that will use the technology in a cautious way without really knowing what direction to take things), and then *firing* off the lesson.

- **Ready, ready, ready . . . fire?** Teachers plan, continue to plan, and then plan some more before maybe deploying the technology. While excess planning may avoid some snags, it is likely more time effective to spend less time planning and normalize the beneficial traits of learning to problem solve and adapt.

- **Ready, fire, aim:** In this approach, teachers spend some time planning but then iteratively implement the technology, readjusting plans each time, thereby moving quickly in a positive direction through actual classroom experiences rather than by advance assumptions.

- **Fire:** Teachers simply use a technology in the classroom without any advance planning. It is still critical and responsible to have *some* advance planning before implementing technology, no matter how adaptable or courageous an educator may be, in order to avoid a different kind of fire (that is, a total lesson failure that could have been easily avoided).

The ready, fire, aim approach requires teachers to understand and model a growth mindset (embracing the idea that skills and abilities are developed and not innate; Dweck, 2016) by being open with students about their own learning and growth. The benefits of diving in with classroom technology and learning *with* students not only outweigh the drawbacks but also create a powerful learning environment where teachers and students feel empowered to share knowledge and skills, make mistakes, and learn on the fly, together.

Holly Moniz and Jackie Clarke are two teachers who embrace Fullan's (2011) advice. In the following sections, you'll see how they utilize technology with a ready, fire, aim approach to support balanced assessment.

Case Study: Holly Moniz

Holly teaches French Immersion and embraces technology in her grades 7–8 classes, not for the sake of the technology itself, but to balance assessment and further learning (see video 4.1).

Here is perhaps the most salient advice Holly offers in this video:

> It's not about the tech . . . about using iMovie or using the camera feature . . . . The lesson is about the great pedagogy that's happening by using the technology to further that and capture it. (Rebooting Assessment, 2021g)

Pause and Reflect

What is your technology-adoption style? Are you more a ready, aim, fire type, or a ready, fire, aim type—or something else? Why do you favor this approach?

Video 4.1: Holly's Technology Journey

Holly explains how she approaches using technology to support learning.

Source: © 2017 by Plan Teach Assess. Used with permission.

Holly's approach is at the apex of a model called *SAMR* (substitution, augmentation, modification, and redefinition; Hamilton, Rosenberg, & Akcaoglu, 2016; Romrell, Kidder, & Wood, 2014), which can be a useful tool to reflect on technology adoption because learning outcomes and not technology adoption itself remain the ultimate measure of success. Holly goes beyond mere *substitution* of paper-and-pencil tasks with technology and also beyond *augmenting* tasks with technology; she redesigns and redefines instruction and learning to provide experiences that could never have been done before. This makes the inherent challenges of using technology worth the effort, and her approach illustrates the power of ready, aim, fire: she is willing to let go of being the expert, and so consequently cultivates a room full of expertise:

> When people hear about tech in education, they automatically say, "I need to do this wonderful lesson about Google Docs," for example. "I need to know everything there is to know about Google Docs, and if I don't know everything as an expert, I am not going to do it." But that's not 21st century education. So 21st century education, as I have learned to evolve over the last eight or nine years of my career, is working with the students and being that facilitator of knowledge. . . .
>
> [Google Docs] is not a program that's been around forever, but we adapted that. We evolved with it. The first time I used it in my classroom last September, I said, "This platform looks really cool. It came out two weeks ago. Let's see what happens." (Rebooting Assessment, 2021g)

Holly's passion for a ready, fire, aim approach in her own classroom makes her a technology leader, and she shows how VOCAL practices are not only rapidly adoptable and adaptable for individual teachers but can also effectively scale and spread within a school environment:

> In terms of taking that learning back to build staff capacity within our school and within, then our school board, it's just working with teachers to discover that themselves. So, not standing up and saying this is why technology is so amazing but coplanning and co-teaching, getting into those classrooms with them, engaging in how this could work. And realizing—and I think this is the biggest thing—when people realize you don't have to be [a technology] expert, it automatically takes away this pressure, which allows the entry into tech to be so much easier. And that happens with teachers; it happens with students. (Rebooting Assessment, 2021g)

Using technology for assessment purposes does not require more time or reduce student interaction. Indeed, it can be quite the opposite, as Holly explains:

> Textbook work? Out the window. Read above; answer ten questions? Out the window. And there's nothing wrong with that. That's what learning used to look like. . . . If you take a look around this classroom, there are no desks. There are no desks because this isn't an individual room. It's structured to be collaborative, and I use the technology to have that collaboration take place. So for example, today [students] . . . were able to engage in discussions about cocreated success criteria for each of the areas of the curriculum for this project, add their ideas, and then we have a community discussion about it. . . . So today, I could have that collaborative discussion and then take their criteria and build them into a checkbric. (Rebooting Assessment, 2021g)

In this way, Holly learned that engaging students is a natural process when they commit to their own learning in a wholehearted way:

> When they've got this checkbric that they're using for their assessment—in this case *for* and *as* learning—they're part of that process. That student voice is there. They know what they are being assessed on. They're passionate about it because they were into it. They have

that buy-in because they created that with me. (Rebooting Assessment, 2021g)

Video 4.2 shows how Holly conducts the approach with her students in the classroom.

Case Study: Jackie Clarke

In video 4.3, Jackie Clarke describes her adoption of technology as a progressive four-step journey: (1) curiosity, (2) commitment, (3) capacity, and (4) confirmation. You'll recognize these milestones from The Teacher-Readiness Scale section (page 27) and from many of the Shift and Share figures throughout this book. At the end of this section, you will have the opportunity to reflect on your own use of technology to boost conversational and observational assessment. Like Jackie, you will be able to move along the continuum from *curiosity* to *commitment* to *capacity* to *confirmation*.

After watching video 4.3, consider where Jackie started:

> I often reflect back on my third year of university. . . . I remember our professor saying to us, "You need to get up and make a presentation." And I thought, "OK, so I'll have a poster board. I'm not gonna use technology because what if it fails on me? . . . So I refused! And I remember thinking, "That's the way to do it because everything needs to work out." So I refused to use technology in my third year of university. (Rebooting Assessment, 2021h)

Relative to the teacher-readiness scale, Jackie is not yet curious, in fact refusing to use technology. But it doesn't take long to nudge that kind of mindset about technology into the realm of curiosity:

> I started seeing the cool things that people were doing, and I thought, "Well, I want to try that! I want to do it!" And of course you stumble and you have a couple of troubles, but you troubleshoot. And that's just like problem solving in any context. (Rebooting Assessment, 2021h)

Jackie's willingness to embrace temporary setbacks exemplifies what makes curiosity about technology the starting place for our teacher-readiness scale. The progression from curiosity to commitment is inevitable:

> In my first two years in [full-day kindergarten] . . . . I just started seeing little snippets

Video 4.2: Cocreating Assessment Criteria With Students

Holly works with students on cocreated assessment criteria.

Source: © 2017 by Plan Teach Assess. Used with permission.

Video 4.3: Jackie's Technology Journey

Jackie discovers the power of technology to capture observations of students and their conversations.

Source: © 2017 by Plan Teach Assess. Used with permission.

of eye-opening moments with kids with technology and just the learning that can be captured. And it's not something that just goes away. It's not just like a picture that you have to infer from. I am able to see documented evidence of the kids' [learning]. (Rebooting Assessment, 2021h)

When teachers begin to see more deeply into student thinking and learning through a balanced approach to assessment that embraces conversations and performances, they move beyond what traditional assessment reveals. From this realization, teachers can begin to build their capacity to maximize the effectiveness of their technology use for balanced assessment:

It just made my assessment practices so much faster because I was able to see in the moment. I wasn't spending hours marking—I was watching, responding, having conversations. The kids and I were talking about it and [then] move on it. It just makes so much more sense. (Rebooting Assessment, 2021h)

As capacity builds and teachers increase their technology-supported use of observation and conversation, experiencing how they can actually save time and provide a more efficient path to effective feedback, they reach the confirmation point on their journey:

Just seeing the spark in their eyes when they watch their video and hearing about showing it to their parents or show . . . to their brother. . . . It's just evidence that keeps proving their learning journey, but then [also] something I can always go back to with them. (Rebooting Assessment, 2021h)

While visiting Jackie's classroom, we saw firsthand how readily students engaged in being their own best assessors (see figure 4.2). About her approach to ready, fire, aim, Jackie says:

Some kids are a little bit more of experts than other kids, so then they pair up and help each other out. Again, it's that whole community feeling. But we have this kind of stuff in norms and expectations of when you are on technology because technology is a privilege and something that can be used really well or can go off. Then we kind of just jumped in and went with it. Once they start to get used to it, they just grab the Chromebook and go. (J. Clarke, personal communication, June 18, 2016)

Figure 4.2:
Viktoria reviewing her
live reading performance.

Source: © 2017 by Plan Teach
Assess. Used with permission.

Lessons From Jackie and Holly

As teachers like Jackie and Holly remind their colleagues, the best way to get started is to jump in! Nevertheless, while we agree wholeheartedly with this message, we have learned that spending some time planning how you will introduce technology into your assessment practice will increase your chances of success as you progress on your own journey from curiosity to confirmation (see figure 4.3).

Three Ways to Try Technology

Like students, teachers are an incredibly diverse group. For example, while most teachers want to know the *whys* of a new approach before they get to the *hows*, some like to dive in to discover their own *whys* (or *why-nots*). Kise (2021) refers to the former as *people who prefer structure and certainty* ("Let me know what to do") and the latter as *people who prefer experience and movement* ("Let me do something"). Still others prefer to follow their own lead (vision and interpretation) or to lead as they learn (question and connection). How teachers approach their own professional growth and learning preferences has a heavy influence on their approach to using IT in the classroom in general, whether or not they use it for assessment purposes.

Whatever your situation, this section outlines a continuum of approaches to using technology for assessment purposes for maximum learning impact and efficiency. Most important, you'll see how all the mobile technology students bring to class supports

Where are you on your technology journey? Self-assess using the teacher-readiness scale. Consider taking one step to the right of where you are comfortable as a next step for your practice.

	Curiosity "I'm curious to learn about . . . ."	**Commitment** "I'm taking steps and beginning to . . . ."	**Capacity** "I'm building on my knowledge and skills for . . . ."	**Confirmation** "I'm proficient at, and helping others to . . . ."
How can digital technology help?	Why technology may or may not have a role in my assessment of student performances and conversations	Collaborate with colleagues who have more expertise to learn to use technology to capture evidence of student performance and conversation	Using technology to capture evidence of student performance and conversation	Use technology to gather, share, and manage evidence of observations and conversations

Commitment-Level Application

Commit to visiting the classroom of a colleague who incorporates technology *in his or her assessment practices*. If you don't know anyone who does this, post a message to your colleagues through email or the school's online forum.

Capacity-Level Application

Working with the colleague you watched or a colleague in your subject area, pick one of your more traditional assessments that needs updating. Tweak the assessment to incorporate student conversation or performance, as well as technology.

Confirmation-Level Application

Ask an administrator if you may share your technology-augmented assessment experience at a future staff meeting.

Figure 4.3: Shift and Share—Ready, fire, aim.

Visit **go.SolutionTree.com/assessment** *for a free reproducible version of this figure.*

your efforts to capture evidence of learning through conversations and performances, not just products—the heart of the VOCAL approach.

The following three approaches effectively support conversations and performances for assessment purposes with differing degrees of commitment to technology, ranging from none at all to extensively integrated.

1. **Unplugged:** Observing and assessing students live with no technology required, although there may be a curiosity about the use of technology

2. **Bring IT:** Letting students do the recording of, sharing of, and reflecting on digital evidence of their learning using their own device

3. **Cloud-based:** Using a variety of cloud-based software and tools for storing, editing, and sharing video content; communicating with students, parents, and other stakeholders; and reporting of summative results (grades)

Whatever your level of confidence with using digital technology, at least one of these approaches will be your sweet spot. If you haven't used much technology in your classroom, going unplugged is a great way to start. As your experience and knowledge increase, you may gradually adopt a bring IT approach or even a cloud-based approach. If you are already comfortable with technology, you may want to begin with one of those two approaches or somewhere in between. There is also a flexible range of commitment as a teacher

to managing the technology versus giving the students that responsibility with their own familiar devices. As your capacity to work with technology grows, so will your balance points on both of these spectrums. Indeed, the ultimate approach is not the most complex one but simply the most appropriate approach for your situation (see figure 4.4).

Unplugged

With the *unplugged approach*, teachers conduct conversations and performance-based assessment tasks without the aid of any technology. They track evidence of learning live, on the fly, without recording anything. For example, access video 4.4, and look for the following as you watch Stephanie Girvan conduct summative interviews regarding a performance task.

- Although we used a camera to record her interview, notice Stephanie does not use any technology herself.

- Watch for *decision points* in the conversation where Stephanie could follow up on a student response or alternatively move on to something else.

- Do you notice any scaffolding, or has differentiated student support been intentionally limited because this is a summative task?

To find a possible starting point for using technology for balanced assessment, highlight the statement in each row that resonates with you. Which row seems most interesting, most effective, simplest, or represents a combination of these factors? Then, commit to a short dialogue with one or more colleagues about which approach they are currently using or might try with you.

	Unplugged	Bring IT	Cloud-Based
What is IT?	Observing and assessing students live with no recording	Students recording, sharing, and reflecting on digital evidence of their learning	Uses free, cloud-based video storage and editing and sharing tools
Upside	No technology to use	Students doing it (mostly)	Maximizes feedback, group sharing, and collaboration
Downside	No evidence available for later, except written notes	Students using their own devices; it's a wild and wonderful world!	Requires competency with cloud software and a stable internet connection
Required technology	No technology available or required	Students using personal or school devices (phones, tablets, laptops, and so on)	Uses personal or school devices (phones, tablets, laptops, and so on) Uses cloud accounts (for example, YouTube, Google Drive)
Teacher skills required	No teacher technology skills required	Students using devices to receive and share files	Requires teacher comfort with capturing and uploading media, using cloud accounts and tools, and so on
Digital evidence capture	None	Students' recording of evidence of learning	Recording evidence of learning and uploading it to the cloud
Digital evidence and assessment	None	Students viewing material on a digital device and sharing with teachers via email or link	Viewing from cloud accounts that allow flexible sharing and self- and peer feedback; assessing at any time and place (school or home); parents accessing, ensuring multiple opportunities for feedback
Digital evidence availability	None	Students viewing or sharing on a digital device and then deleting it	Accessing ongoing, long-term flexible recorded content; allowing pausing and rewatching; maintaining evidence of learning long-term for student portfolios or accountability

Figure 4.4: Shift and Share—Three ways to approach IT.

*Visit **go.SolutionTree.com/assessment** for a free reproducible version of this figure.*

Although the interview in video 4.4 (page 84) shows a teacher-student summative task, the unplugged approach works equally well for student-student tasks and formative assessments. Going unplugged also allows teachers who haven't yet reached the curiosity stage in their readiness for technology adoption to be fully present and attentive to the task and feedback process. While there won't be any recordings of the task itself, this does constitute a significant step toward balanced assessment, albeit in a technology-free way.

Now, consider video 4.5, which features Helen Hills, whose class features prominently in chapter 2 (page 34) and chapter 3 (page 54). This video shows Helen observing students conducting a novel seminar as part of her summative assessment. The following highlight some key contextual takeaways and look-fors with Helen's approach.

- No technology is incorporated or required in Helen's approach.

- The students are performing this task as part of an end-of-course assessment. Do they seem at ease?

- Helen has given the students previous opportunities throughout the school year to practice and hone these skills, understand the assessment criteria, and learn how to participate successfully in a group task.

- Notice this is a relatively quiet hallway just outside the classroom. The rest of the class is working, unsupervised, in the classroom. As we detailed in chapter 3, Helen has put significant emphasis on building classroom community, trust, and independence.

Video 4.5: Unplugged Group Observation (by Teacher)

Helen observes students conducting a novel seminar as part of her final evaluation assessment.

Source: © 2017 by Plan Teach Assess. Used with permission.

As you get more comfortable with the unplugged approach, you may feel motivated to begin using technology to record a conversation or performance. There are many good reasons for capturing evidence, including the following.

- Keeping digital evidence of student achievement for accountability

- Capturing content for student reflection or for their portfolios

- Allowing for self- or peer review and feedback at any time or place

- Increasing flexibility for implementing assessment and grading at any time or place

- Sharing evidence of learning online for parents to access

- Pausing and rewatching a performance to ensure accurate observation of conversations and performances

Bring IT

It's common in many districts for students to bring handheld technology (smartphones, tablets, and so on) to class and know how to use it, particularly at the secondary level. So the *bring IT approach* lets students do the recording and sharing for you. Especially for teachers already in bring your own device (BYOD)-friendly schools, simply asking students to document their *own* evidence of interviews or performances is an effective and efficient strategy to inject more assessment of conversations and performances into your assessment routines. This enables triangulation, as described in chapter 1 (page 12) and chapter 2. Like assessment *as* learning, where students are directly involved, responsible, and committed to their own assessment, involving students in the use of technology helps them develop initiative, problem-solving skills, and the same responsible, committed qualities.

Whether or not your school is BYOD-friendly, it's possible for students to record observations and conversations for you, freeing you to do what you do best: teach and support students' learning. In this way, the bring IT approach remains a simple way to begin using VOCAL strategies.

In video 4.6, Jamie Mitchell first has students practice responding to a question orally, then receiving feedback from their partner, and finally recording another trial run. All this is in preparation for doing a teacher-student interview so students develop skills and a level of comfort in sharing their mathematics understanding in conversation and using their own technology to record evidence along the way.

Ideally, by this point (and no matter where you are in your assessment or technology journey), you can see yourself somewhere in these options. There are many ranges of practice including: the use (or not) of technology, the involvement (or not) of students in technology, the capture (or not) of classroom performances and conversations, and the involvement (or not) of students in their own assessment. The key is for teachers and students alike to embrace challenge and celebrate mistakes as part of discovering deeper and more engaging learning experiences for students.

Cloud-Based

The last of the three approaches to using technology to support balanced assessment expands the scope of teachers' technology toolkits to include cloud-based (web-based or internet-based) services like Google Drive, YouTube, and so on to improve and deepen assessment

**Video 4.6:
Student-Student Interview**

Jamie's ninth-grade students use peer interviews to practice mathematics.

Source: © 2017 by Plan Teach Assess. Used with permission.

for learning. Not only is the content (documents, spreadsheets, presentations, audio, video, and so on) stored and accessed in the cloud, but the tools to manipulate and edit that content are all also cloud-based. Learning to use these platforms falls beyond the scope of this work (not to mention the fast pace of software updates means any such direction might quickly fall out of date), but you can use the following links to learn more about cloud technology.

- **Google for Education products (https:// bit.ly/3ufpBYG):** This resource offers links to getting started with a host of Google products educators commonly use.

- **Google for Education Fundamentals Training (https://bit.ly/2POQ00t):** This online class for teachers provides thirteen units of instruction to support teacher adoption of a variety of technology tools and practices.

- **Microsoft Educator Center (https:// education.microsoft.com):** Microsoft offers a host of tools at their Educator Center, including specialized training for teachers to get started using technology for learning.

- **Teachers YouTube channel (https:// youtube.com/user/teachers):** This YouTube channel acts as a repository of educational content.

Many teachers and districts realize the power of a cloud-based approach (Bedell, 2014). In most cases, these technology platforms eliminate the hassle of tracking software versions (because the cloud updates automatically), and there is little or nothing to install or get a license for. Furthermore, such platforms rarely become inaccessible because of compatibility issues with the device you're using, although internet or network service interruptions can certainly interrupt access. For this reason, education, consumer, and corporate users alike flock to online platforms for communications, file storage and sharing, collaboration around documents, and using video for a variety of purposes (Cortez, 2017). And this was happening before the COVID-19

global pandemic forced both teachers and students to learn outside classroom walls (Hansen, 2020).

Given growing district and school adoption of services with low cost of implementation, accessibility on almost any device, and ease of use (Hansen, 2020), you will likely be faced with the option (or requirement) to use the cloud as a teacher. Whatever your own personal comfort level with cloud technology, it is likely that at some point in your life, you have already recorded video on a smartphone or at least accessed video content on YouTube. These two basic skills are all you really need to start your journey toward a cloud-based approach to using technology for balanced assessment.

Regardless of whether you have access to district-provided tools (such as a feature-rich LMS), or you create a personal educator account to access services from providers like YouTube or Google Drive, a growing number of tools enables the recording of learning, puts that evidence in the cloud, and manages distribution and sharing of that content to enhance your assessment practices in the many ways you've seen throughout this book.

As with the unplugged and bring IT approaches, and as the Shift and Share reflects in figure 4.5, a cloud-based approach can balance and transform assessment by using conversations and performances. For example, video 4.7 (page 90) features students reviewing a recording of their own performance task, utilizing multiple devices at the same time. As you watch this video, consider the following look-fors.

- Notice how students are making use of multiple devices with shared access to data. In this case, they are accessing a cloud-based recording of their performance task, and then using the other device to access a document with assessment criteria also stored in the cloud.

- Watch the students reflect on their performance and connect it directly to the criteria.

Whatever your comfort level with gathering evidence of student conversations and performances, hopefully, you have had a chance to review different approaches and decide what resonates with you.

- To what degree have you incorporated the use of technology for assessment in your classroom?
- Is there an approach you would like to try or are already using that you might extend or deepen?

Use the statements in the teacher-readiness scale to help you in your technology adoption.

	Curiosity *"I'm curious to learn about...."*	Commitment *"I'm taking steps and beginning to...."*	Capacity *"I'm building on my knowledge and skills for...."*	Confirmation *"I'm proficient at, and helping others to...."*
How do I assess learning using balanced assessment?	At least one simple way to gather evidence through observations and conversations	Gather evidence of learning through observations and conversations	Gathering evidence through observations and conversations	Gather, share, and involve students in assessing evidence through observations and conversations
How do I use digital technology to implement balanced assessment?	How to watch and assess student performances or interviews live without technology	Allow students to use technology to capture evidence of their learning	Using cloud technology to capture, share, and manage evidence of students' learning	Use technology in a variety of ways to capture evidence of students' learning

Commitment-Level Application

Pair students and have one partner record a short performance of or conversation with the other, then switch. Let them watch their own performance and self-assess using clear criteria. Request permission to share these recordings in class and talk about them. With student permission, keep a few exemplars for next time, and use the videos to show future students what an excellent quality performance or conversation looks and sounds like.

Capacity-Level Application

Make a tally of assessment tasks for your curriculum according to whether they are a product, conversation, or performance. If you find a significant majority of one type or a complete lack of one or more types, rebalance by revising some of the tasks, perhaps incorporating technology to redesign or reimagine the task.

Confirmation-Level Application

Develop a brief online or live professional learning session for the teachers in your school to outline the benefits of using technology to support assessment. You may wish to base it on the Shift and Share from figure 4.4 (page 85), which charts the three approaches to using technology.

Figure 4.5: Shift and Share—Increasing technology adoption for balanced assessment.

*Visit **go.SolutionTree.com/assessment** for a free reproducible version of this figure.*

Video 4.7: Student Group Reflection

Students use multiple cloud-connected devices to assess their group's performance.

Source: © 2017 by Plan Teach Assess. Used with permission.

- Think about how this example of group self-assessment might translate to an individual self-assessment, peer assessment, or teacher assessment.

This was a group self-assessment, and the possibilities for capturing, sharing, collaborating, and assessing are limitless when cloud tools are employed with conversations and performance-based observations to reveal student learning. Beyond all use of technology, the most important factor is to nurture rich learning experiences for students that not only involve them but engage their minds and hearts fully. Assessing all this will absolutely require a balance of diverse assessment practices as outlined in previous chapters.

Questions About Using Technology to Support Assessment

The following sections address common questions we receive from teachers about using technology to benefit assessment.

How Do I Plan for Technology Challenges?

As we've mentioned throughout this chapter, perhaps the biggest obstacle to using technology in the classroom isn't the potential for something to go wrong but the *fear* of how something might go wrong. Educators have all given or sat through a presentation with a technology fail. Technological glitches are a common and often frustrating experience (Zetlin, 2016). Yet glitches are actually a natural, necessary, and useful aspect of learning and growth. According to growth mindset expert Carol S. Dweck (2016), embracing challenges and persisting in the face of setbacks lead to higher levels of achievement and a greater sense of free will. It's a core aspect of her vision of a growth mindset. At the same time, some advance planning and thinking can help you avoid certain setbacks. The greatest challenge is to find the right balance of getting *ready* and taking *aim* versus *firing away* (see figure 4.6).

this is your comfort zone

this is where the **magic** happens

Figure 4.6: Growth happens outside your comfort zone.

Planning for challenges doesn't start with anticipating challenges but with adjusting your mindset to see and *invite* challenges as a necessary component of growth. With this mindset, you can prepare more effectively without overplanning. The key is to avoid the most common pitfalls. The following are some key factors that can support or hamper your implementation of digital technology in the classroom.

- Classroom environment
- Wireless network quality in your school
- Availability of devices (district-provided or student-owned)
- Access to software and services
- District and school technology policies (such as BYOD, online content filtering, and so on)

In the following sections, we examine some planning considerations for each factor and then consider quick fixes for the most common challenges.

Classroom Environment

A classroom is certainly not a recording studio, but the challenge of finding spaces for conducting interviews and having students perform for balanced assessment is easy to overcome (see figure 4.7). In the classroom, set up a desk in a quiet corner for interviews or direct students how to rearrange space for small-group recordings, such as having each group face a corner to avoid clutter in the shot and minimize cross noise.

Figure 4.7: Address the challenge of finding a quiet space for observation.

Source: © 2017 Plan Teach Assess. Used with permission. Used with permission.

If you can use the hallway outside your classroom or have access to a nearby unused room or outdoor space, you have even more options. Setting up

conversation and performance stations that take advantage of additional spaces increases your flexibility to conduct balanced assessments while minimizing classroom clatter (the inevitable noise that results from a classroom full of active learning and assessment experiences).

Even if you can't use extra spaces to minimize the noise in your classroom, remember that teachers incorporating VOCAL approaches do not find noise to be problematic, even with multiple groups in one room. Keep recording devices close to the action, particularly for interviews or small-group tasks, which will allow you and students to use lower voices, keeping a ceiling on just how loud things get.

The placement of recording devices (smartphones, tablets, and so on) requires less planning than how you arrange space, but it's still worth considering. Tablets and laptops as recording devices have an advantage because they can often act as their own stands. Teachers and students just need a flat surface to set them on (usually a desk rather than a stool or something that can be knocked over) that keeps the conversation or performance central in the frame. If you or students need the device up higher, stack something underneath. If you or students are using smartphone cameras to record, you can use similar materials to prop up the device. Or, you might ask the school to invest in one or more tripods that support mounting a smartphone.

Even in the absence of an ideal flat surface or smartphone mount, it's always possible for teachers or students to simply hold up the device while recording. This will introduce some movement in the video, but again, what's important is capturing evidence of learning, not if the recording is suitable for entry in film festivals.

Use figure 4.8 (page 92) as a checklist as you consider options for how to maximize your use of classroom space, and for what materials you'll use for recording conversations and performances.

What spaces are available to record evidence of learning?

☐ Quiet corners

☐ Hallway

☐ An unused or currently empty room

☐ Outdoor space

☐ Other spaces (list): _____

_____

_____

What devices (school-owned or BYOD) and materials will you and students use to record evidence of learning?

☐ Laptops

☐ Tablets

☐ Video cameras

☐ Smartphones

☐ Tripods or other camera mounts

☐ Desktops and tables

☐ Other classroom materials (list): _____

_____

_____

Figure 4.8: Quick fixes for classroom recording.

*Visit **go.SolutionTree.com/assessment** for a free reproducible version of this figure.*

Wireless Network Quality

A weak or unreliable wireless network impacts both the tech-savvy and the tech-avoiders. The signal strength, speed, and accessibility of the wireless network in your classroom will likely be the most important aspects of how reliably you can use a cloud-based approach to support your use of recorded conversations or performances. Uploading videos to cloud storage to access later or share with others, plus watching those uploaded videos, requires a reliable and fast network.

In many schools and communities, this is not a problem. Both wired (such as cable and fiber) and wireless (such as cellular and satellite) internet providers get faster and more reliable every year, as do the site-based Wi-Fi networks that interface with them. However, it's still common for schools and

homes to have less reliable Wi-Fi networks. Without a suitable network, you may have trouble using a cloud-based approach, since any recordings taken will only be available on the device that captured them, which may suggest a bring IT approach. In this case, your first action could be to check with school IT staff. It's possible there is a correctable problem they can address to improve students' access to the cloud while in your classroom. If not, you can still utilize a bring IT or an unplugged approach to great effect. Furthermore, if you or students can't reliably upload recorded evidence of learning inside the school building, that doesn't necessarily mean you or the students can't do so later from home or another location with more reliable connectivity.

If your network is usable but slow, you might consider reducing the number of devices trying to access it at once. For example, if every student in your class is accessing the network at the same time, ask students to work in groups with just one device for each group actively accessing the network. Additionally, media can be stored and shared on the devices themselves, meaning that students simply pass along a device with a recording on it to share with their teacher. This approach works with students if the classroom community is developed to the point where there is sufficient trust to share devices. Use figure 4.9 as a checklist as you consider how to approach your use of wireless connectivity in your classroom.

Availability of Devices

Obviously, recording student conversations and performances for balanced assessment requires a device to record with. Although you can use one or more dedicated video cameras for video recording (as noted throughout this book), there is no need to acquire one. Smartphone cameras, tablet-based cameras, and webcams common to laptops are more than adequate. More important, it is generally easier to share and send media for a cloud-based approach when you capture those records directly to a network-connected device such as a smartphone.

The extent to which you can adopt a bring IT or cloud-based approach depends on the availability and procurement options of media-capable devices. Schools that issue one device per student or have a strong BYOD program in place make it easy for teachers to adopt a bring IT approach. This does require teachers and students to commit to certain classroom agreements around the use of technology, but such agreements are well worth the effort, and we explore those in more detail in the District and School Technology Policies section (page 95).

Where there is a limited number of devices for students to use, organize conversation- and performance-based assessments around group work that enables students to share those devices productively (see figure 4.10). Even one device can be effective for supporting balanced assessment if you set up a single recording station in your classroom and identify the assessment tasks in your curriculum that station is best equipped to support. Remember, having less technology doesn't preclude using VOCAL strategies; it just can mean you use available technology even more efficiently through rotation and sharing.

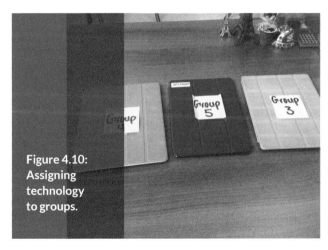

Figure 4.10: Assigning technology to groups.

Source: © 2017 Plan Teach Assess. Used with permission. Used with permission.

Use figure 4.11 as a checklist as you consider how to approach your use of wireless connectivity in your classroom.

If wireless connectivity isn't working or sufficient to support your cloud-based approach, what quick fixes should you try?

- ☐ Check with school IT support staff about improving network accessibility.
- ☐ Limit simultaneous use of devices or stagger when students upload.
- ☐ Change locations to where the network signal is stronger.
- ☐ Watch recordings on the device that recorded them.
- ☐ Go unplugged.
- ☐ Other (list): _____
  _____
  _____

Figure 4.9: Quick fixes for challenges with wireless networks.

Visit *go.SolutionTree.com/assessment* for a free reproducible version of this figure.

Assess your options for using recording devices to record evidence of learning in your classroom.

- ☐ There are enough devices for each student to use their own. (Embrace BYOD!)
- ☐ There are a limited number of recording devices for students to use. To support their productive use of available devices, set up the following.
  - ☐ Set up one or more stations for recording.
  - ☐ Have students work in groups while sharing devices.
- ☐ The devices my students can use for recording include the following.
  - ☐ Dedicated video cameras
  - ☐ Smartphones
  - ☐ Tablets
  - ☐ Laptops (including Chromebooks)
  - ☐ Other (list): _____
- ☐ Other considerations (list): _____
  _____
  _____

Figure 4.11: Quick fixes for using recording devices.

Visit *go.SolutionTree.com/assessment* for a free reproducible version of this figure.

Access to Software and Services

We sometimes find that teachers assume a VOCAL approach requires specialized, expensive video-editing software, subscriptions for cloud services, and so on, but these are unnecessary. While it is possible to spend significant funds on installed software licenses, subscriptions, and more, teachers can establish and sustain a cloud-based VOCAL approach to balanced assessment with a few free online services, device apps, and so on. These options include numerous additional benefits, such as seamless updates, shallow learning curves, and low barriers to entry.

Most modern software can be used without having to think about how the software itself works, and this holds true in the classroom. For example, students recording on their phones and uploading have almost no need to be concerned with the software that makes it all work. There is an axiom in software development known as the *Pareto Principle*, which states that 80 percent of results come from just 20 percent of effort, and the remaining 20 percent of results come from 80 percent of effort (Vasylyna, 2011). In terms of the classroom, 80 percent of your functionality for supporting recorded conversations and performances for balanced assessment will come from just 20 percent of software features. By avoiding more complex software and services and sticking to baseline features, you and students will avoid the hassles that come with using expensive and complicated software.

Often, your district or school will already have done most of the work for you by providing both teacher and student access to cloud-based accounts and software that enable online communication, file storage and sharing, and more. For staff and students, this is *the* place to start (unless you are a technology maverick who is self-supporting). The advantage of district-provided accounts and services is the elevated support teachers will have from school IT staff and that these accounts and services come with student-appropriate privacy and protection.

However, even where there are no district- or school-provided cloud-based accounts, teachers can successfully create personal accounts using educator labels, such as "Mr. D.'s Class," to support a cloud-based approach to balanced assessment. (Note, you should not require students to sign up for their own personal accounts, where the terms of use or your board policies will be violated.)

> "
> The Pareto Principle states that 20% of efforts bring 80% of results, and the other 80% of efforts bring only 20% of results. The first person to discover this pattern was Vilfredo Pareto, an economist from Italy. He concluded that 80% of all property in Italy belonged to only 20% of the population. He also suggested that this pattern could be found in many other areas. (Vasylyna, 2011)

To begin, it's important to note that all the tools you and students need to capture video evidence of learning are already on the device used to record that content. The camera app on these devices is all you need. Many devices provide tools for making simple edits to recorded video (though video editing is unnecessary for teachers and students to review and assess learning). However, to store and share files and communicate online, and so on, you will need access to cloud-based services. We suggest reviewing the options listed earlier in this chapter (see the Cloud-Based section, page 87). There are strong options to get you started, but we encourage you to explore all of your options.

In any case, the most critical tools teachers and students need are for *capturing* the video and *sharing* that recorded video. Additional tools to *edit* video, support communication (for conversation, discussion, and so on), conduct virtual classrooms, and so on can also be very useful. However, none of them is essential for supporting a VOCAL approach. Use figure 4.12 as a checklist as you consider how to approach your use of wireless connectivity in your classroom.

District and School Technology Policies

Internet-access agreements, software-usage policies, and hardware-distribution processes will all positively or negatively impact your use of technology for balanced assessment. If there has been a history of restrictive policymaking in your district or school (cumbersome network-access requirements, unreasonable internet-content filtering, restrictions that block access to useful cloud-based tools and services, locked-down devices, and so on), then you may find the unplugged or bring IT approaches necessary in the short term. However, that doesn't mean you can't open a discussion with school and district staff about how to update these policies to reflect the needs of an online world filled with online learners. If you teach in a district or school with a balanced approach to its technology policy (that is, one with a focus on student needs), you will likely find your school or district's IT department a strong source of information and support for your needs.

Pause and Reflect

How could you personally influence or provide input about a school or district IT policy?

Unfortunately, sometimes district and school IT policies are attempts to avoid what we call *type 1* issues that ultimately lead to *type 2* issues, as the following explains.

- **Type 1:** These issues include serious problems that can arise wherever teachers and students have access to internet-connected technology, such as security breaches, student misbehavior, and so on that most

Assess your options for using recording devices in your classroom for recording evidence of learning.

- ☐ Where can I obtain access to software and services to support balanced assessment?
  - ☐ District or school
  - ☐ Personal accounts
  - ☐ Both
- ☐ What software and services do I currently have access to?
  - ☐ Video recording software (list): _____
  - ☐ Cloud-based file storage and sharing (list): _____
  - ☐ Cloud-based communication tools (list): _____
  - ☐ Other (list): _____
- ☐ What software and services do I not currently have access to but want to investigate using?
  - ☐ Video recording software (list): _____
  - ☐ Cloud-based file storage and sharing (list): _____
  - ☐ Cloud-based communication tools (list): _____
  - ☐ Other (list): _____

Figure 4.12: Quick fixes for using software to support balanced assessment.

Visit *go.SolutionTree.com/assessment* for a free reproducible version of this figure.

restrictive but well-intended technology policies are designed to prevent.

- **Type 2:** These issues arise where restrictive technology policies prevent or inhibit actual learning or learning opportunities.

When technology policies are skewed too heavily toward preventing type 1 issues (incidents), they cause a disproportionate number of type 2 issues (not learning). In a progressive district, technical and educational staff alike will understand it is inevitable that a small number of type 1 issues will occur as a consequence of having a relatively simple, unencumbered system. In fact, the presence of *some* incidents can be seen as a positive indicator of a balanced approach to technology policy. The goal is to minimize and reduce risk, not to completely eliminate it. If learning is a district and school's primary focus, then policies that align with that goal will be most effective and transparent to teachers and students.

Where policies are highly restrictive, consider how you might provide feedback and input to principals, IT leaders, and district staff on how policies might evolve and improve over time to better support learning. In *Growing Global Digital Citizens*, education experts and consultants Lee Watanabe Crockett and Andrew Churches (2018) offer numerous ideas to schools for effectively implementing digital citizenship agreements to support students' technology use. At the classroom level, Angela Watson (n.d.), a National Board Certified teacher and founder of Due Season Press and Educational Services, offers useful guidance for teachers on supporting productive use of devices in a BYOD classroom.

How Do I Get Unstuck?

With some planning in place, your ready, fire, aim approach moves to *fire*. Try something, see what happens, make adjustments, and dive in again. Learning is like that! And while the advance planning (we describe in the previous set of sections) is helpful, taking the leap and being a co-learner

with students not only help teachers develop their capacity to live with the uncertainty that is life in the classroom but also model qualities of resilience and problem solving that are key for students to develop.

When inevitable glitches occur, do not overreact to them or set yourself up as the sole source of solutions. In fact, part of your job as a learning facilitator is to grow your students' ability to learn and act autonomously, gradually releasing responsibility for learning tasks to them, as you have seen throughout this book. So, react calmly to technology problems and with an investigative mindset. Troubleshooting such problems is largely about assessing what issues *could* be causing the problem and testing and eliminating each until you've found the problem's source. Your students, who are often tech savvy, can assist you in this process. We suggest sharing and posting the following *TASTE* strategy for getting unstuck in your classroom.

1. **Try another way:** Try using a different device or software tool. Reboot the device. If all else fails, go unplugged.

2. **Ask a friend:** Students typically understand how to use their own personal devices and can often help peers, even across platforms.

3. **Search it:** As the VOCAL approach employs cloud-based tools, there are often online tutorials, help and support resources, and so on. Furthermore, if you or a student experience an error, it's likely someone else has too. Try a simple internet search based on received error messages or a description of the problem. Odds are you will find someone else who had the same problem and found a solution.

4. **Take a break:** Technology can be infuriating, and no one's patience is unlimited. Take a breath and a break (a day or two sometimes) to reset your mind

and thereby let solutions be much more apparent. It may be necessary to look for solutions outside class time rather than distract from students' learning.

5. **Engage your brain:** After a break and a chance to refresh, start by asking yourself, "What would a wise, resourceful person do right now, in this situation?" Barring extreme circumstances, every problem has a solution. If the problem is related to school-provided resources, contact your IT staff. If it's related to personal software or devices, the device's owner may need to access or contact help resources from the provider.

Pause and Reflect

- Where is my comfort level in using technology with a bring IT or cloud-based approach?

- What software do I need or want?

- How comfortable am I diving into using new technology with students?

How Do I Store Digital Evidence of Learning?

In this chapter and throughout this book, we outline the benefits of recording and storing digital evidence of student conversations and performances for the purposes of balanced assessment. Although an unplugged approach does not use recorded content, and a bring IT approach doesn't specifically require keeping or sharing recorded content, a cloud-based approach depends on having somewhere to put captured evidence of learning where teachers, students, and other stakeholders can access it. The numerous benefits to maintaining recordings of assessment evidence over time include the following.

- Accountability for evaluations

- Ease of incorporating multiple assessors (teachers, students, and peers)

- Capacity for assessment tasks and feedback to happen asynchronously (shifted to any place or time)

- Option to pause, rewatch, slow down, and even annotate evidence of learning

- More teacher time for instruction when students do the recording

First, it's important to address the elephant in the room. Anything you or students record digitally and put into the cloud is at least *potentially* permanent and public. Cloud storage is intended to be secure, but everyone has seen evidence of even secure platforms being hacked and private information leaked. And everyone knows anything posted publicly to social media can live forever in one form or another. So, it's important to recognize that anyone at any time has the potential to access anything captured with technology. However, there are some ways to store, organize, and access digital material with minimal risk and effort. The following sections address our suggestions (from the simplest to the most complex) for taking maximum advantage of ways to share evidence of learning in the cloud to support balanced assessment.

On-Device Storage and Sharing

The highest keep-it-super-simple approach is to store all media on the device which records it. This is basically a bring IT approach that precludes the need for cloud access. This may be more necessary for larger files, which are not quickly transferable (especially over slow networks) or that exceed file-size sharing maximums. Watching recorded videos on the device is also necessary if district-provided devices are periodically reset and stored files are removed.

Watching a video on the recording device, usually soon after making the recording, can happen in class on the fly or at a convenient time soon after, as long as that particular device is still accessible.

For example, individual students using BYOD will have access in class and after school. Small- or large-group recordings that remain on the device usually require viewing in class where small groups watch it on the device or hook up the device to a projector for a whole-class review of a performance.

The drawback of this strategy is that many of the advantages we list at the outset of this section are lost when teachers do not have convenient long-term access to the content or device. This isn't a factor if the device used to record evidence of student learning belongs to the teacher, as evidence is consolidated in one place without any need to transfer files. However, a one-device approach to balanced assessment also limits the kinds of conversations and performances teachers can assess. For this reason, the cloud-based methods described in the following sections are usually preferable for maximizing balanced assessment opportunities.

Basic Sharing

One step up from gathering around one device or screen is to record content on one device and then use sharing tools common to most recording devices to distribute the captured content. This involves using the ubiquitous Share icon on virtually every media app on every smartphone or tablet (and even most laptops). Share icons typically resemble those depicted in figure 4.13. Tapping them usually brings up a list of options for how to share a media file with someone else (teacher or student), such as through text messages, email addresses, via a social media upload, and so on.

While a Share icon provides convenient methods for sharing recorded content, it's usually simple to use a device's text messaging, email, or other media apps. For example, you might provide students with your district email address, modeling for students how they can attach a media file to an email message and send it to you (see figure 4.14).

Cloud Storage

Unsurprisingly, the ideal way to share evidence of student learning is to use the cloud to store and share recordings. Teachers and students can do this through a Share icon on their device, posting recordings to a cloud-based service like Google Drive or Apple iCloud, a video-hosting platform like YouTube, or a district or school LMS. The latter option is becoming increasingly common. In a survey of school districts, IT departments project that 80 percent of their environments will include cloud-based technology by the end of 2022 (Castelo, 2020). As K–12 schools increasingly embrace cloud-based LMS and even third-party platforms like YouTube and Google Drive, classrooms will have outstanding media capture and management tools available on any device at any time. Even where districtwide implementations are still evolving, individual teachers may still use these tools effectively and safely.

Note that a cloud-based approach is the natural outcome for teachers who start their technology journey unplugged, or with some form of the bring IT approach, particularly if they are already comfortable using technology to support learning. Ultimately, cloud storage provides the best medium for teachers who want to regularly and powerfully incorporate conversations and performances into their balanced assessments.

Pause and Reflect

The idea of students taking a written test (a product-based assessment) and not recording their work for the assessor would be pointless. Are assessments through conversations and performances any different?

One advantage of cloud-based storage is that students and teachers are already familiar with the platforms through using them in their personal lives. Many people use cloud storage to share documents with colleagues or photos with family. They create hobbyist pages on Pinterest or sell household items on eBay. Going from consumer and personal applications that involve cloud storage to creating a dedicated space for teachers and students to post and share recorded evidence of learning can be as simple as creating an account with Google (Drive), Microsoft (OneDrive), Apple (iCloud), or Dropbox and giving students access to that online space. Once set up, teachers can configure many devices and device-based apps to automatically upload content to that space without any user intervention required.

At that point, teachers can easily share and review content with any number of people, including students and parents. For example, teachers may allow parents to access classroom observations of their children through link sharing. Teachers might post student videos to YouTube using an unlisted setting, which makes the videos only accessible to people who have a link. Similarly, platforms like YouTube offer private settings in which uploaded content is *only* shareable with specific, named people (classmates, parents, and so on).

ePortfolios

Although basic cloud storage is extremely useful for implementing balanced assessment, teachers can take learning and assessment a step further by supporting students in building an ePortfolio. An *ePortfolio* is a student-owned and operated online workspace to keep, reflect on, and share evidence of learning (recorded

Figure 4.13: Common Share icons found on smartphones, tablets, and other devices.

Figure 4.14: Students access recorded content to share with their teacher.

Source: © 2017 Plan Teach Assess. Used with permission. Used with permission.

conversations and performances as well as products). In our experience, when students take ownership of curating, assessing, and showcasing their work, the result is inevitably a greater commitment to learning, an increase in metacognitive skills, as well as increased feelings of self-efficacy.

Although there may be some ePortfolio functionality embedded in your district intranet or LMS, generic tools can also provide essential ePortfolio functionality. As we noted earlier with the Pareto Principle, 80 percent of the benefit of using technology tools comes from 20 percent of available features, so having a dedicated ePortfolio platform is unnecessary for most classrooms. Look for a system that can provide storage, retrieval, and flexible sharing, with online feedback and shared document editing as a bonus (see figure 4.15). Common school-adopted platforms like Google for Education, FreshGrade, Blackboard, and

Desire2Learn all provide the necessary components to build compelling ePortfolios. (Visit https://bit .ly/3Dtd348 for a curated collection of apps and websites for ePortfolios.)

Examining the sophisticated levels of functionality and specific features for each of these platforms is beyond the scope of this resource. However, we cannot overstate their capacity to empower teachers, parents, and students to collaborate in gathering, sharing, and analyzing evidence of learning and, perhaps most important, to transform how all stakeholders view grading and reporting.

While an ePortfolio will hold assignments and projects students have completed throughout their year or school career, it isn't just a repository of stuff. It is a dynamic window into the learning process. An ePortfolio facilitates the sharing of feedback from

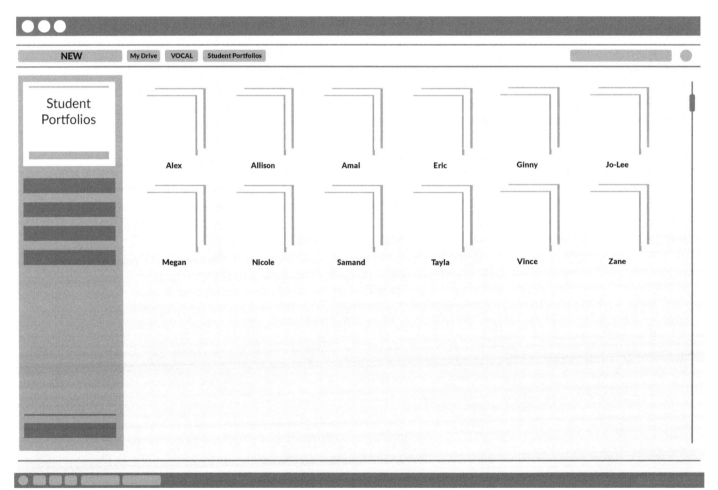

Figure 4.15: A mockup of a cloud-based storage platform with folders for each student.

multiple sources—self, peer, teacher, parent—and shows the corresponding revisions students make. The concept of ensuring students have multiple opportunities to show their learning takes on new meaning when they can go back, revise, and refine their work over time, with teachers, peers, and parents able to see how a piece of work improves version after version as students progress along a learning path.

Students always own their ePortfolios, although teachers also have the ability to access portfolio contents and provide feedback. Parents or guardians can follow their child's work throughout the year, in real time, without the need for ongoing manual sharing or sending. (See Direction 1: *Push* Communication Gives Way to *Pull* Communication on page 128 in chapter 6.)

If you are considering implementing ePortfolios, why not take one more step and have the students do it themselves? Students in almost any grade, including primary classes, can create their own ePortfolios, especially with the added safety and support of a district-adopted LMS or other cloud-based platform.

In video 4.8, Holly, who has a case study in this chapter and again in chapter 5 (page 104), describes how cloud-based storage and tools help her to manage not only the sharing of tasks and assessment criteria with students but also the large number of student files created in response. She also touches on the additional benefits of cloud technology for ePortfolios, team teaching, and communicating information to parents.

Video 4.8: Interview on the Use of Cloud Tools to Manage Video

Holly describes here adoption of cloud-based tools.

Source: © 2017 Plan Teach Assess. Used with permission.

ePortfolios ultimately exemplify the principles of assessment *as* learning (Earl, 2013). Whether or not students create their ePortfolios, having them manage their own evidence builds skills of discernment and helps students more deeply understand success criteria. As students curate particular items for their portfolios and share them with peers, teachers, and parents, they come to a better understanding of their talents, their potential, and areas for growth (see figure 4.16, page 102).

The use of ePortfolios edges into the realm of communication about student learning, except, in this case, it is the student rather than the teacher who is directly involved in the curation and review of the learning evidence and subsequent communication. Reflect on the following scale, this time from the perspective of supporting students in being their own best assessors.

	Curiosity "I'm curious to learn about . . . ."	Commitment "I'm taking steps and beginning to . . . ."	Capacity "I'm building on my knowledge and skills for . . . ."	Confirmation "I'm proficient at, and helping others to . . . ."
How do I support students in curating and sharing their own learning using digital evidence?	How to help students capture evidence from observations and conversations to improve communication with teachers and parents about their learning	Require students to select and review evidence from observations and conversations to improve communication with teachers and parents about their learning	Supporting students in presenting and sharing evidence from observations and conversations to improve communication with teachers and parents about their learning	Enable students to become independent and effective assessors of their own learning and communicating this to others through ePortfolios

Commitment-Level Application

Inspire yourself: take a walk to the staff room and talk to any art-loving teacher about the purpose and passion behind portfolios, which are integral to learning and assessment in the arts. Then, consider the application of ePortfolios to your own teaching.

Capacity-Level Application

Pick one of the following links to find out more about ePortfolios, and find out if your district or school supports one of them. Dive in!

- Student Portfolio Apps and Websites (https://commonsense.org/education/top-picks/student-portfolio-apps -and-websites)

- Tools for Creating Digital Student Portfolios (https://edutopia.org/article/tools-creating-digital-student -portfolios)

- Student Portfolios as an Assessment Tool (https://educationworld.com/a_curr/columnists/mcdonald /mcdonald025.shtml)

Confirmation-Level Application

Ask students to select (or select yourself) some diverse examples of key tasks from existing ePortfolios. Upload these examples to an accessible online platform for future students to use as guideposts for creating even better work and learning more deeply.

Figure 4.16: Shift and Share—Learning about ePortfolios.

Visit **go.SolutionTree.com/assessment** *for a free reproducible version of this figure.*

Key Messages

As you reflect on this chapter, we urge you to focus on the following key messages.

1. Incorporating technology into the assessment of conversations and performances deepens insights into learning, enables self-assessment, saves time, and allows for the preservation of evidence of learning.

2. When adopting new technology practices, you can find a healthy balance of comfort level and challenge by using a ready, fire, aim approach.

3. Challenges such as a lack of hardware and software, poor network quality, and restrictive policies inevitably occur, but are also an important and necessary part of the learning and change process.

4. Teachers and students can store digital evidence of learning in a variety of ways in order to provide feedback to improve learning and accountability, and to facilitate communication among students, teachers, and parents.

How Do I Use the VOCAL Approach to Improve Learning?

In this chapter, we examine how the VOCAL approach is critical to the formative assessment purpose (assessment *for* learning) and how, if a teacher employs handheld technology to capture digital evidence of student learning during the teaching-and-learning process, the results can be remarkable. Because digital evidence of learning (through captured conversations and performances) is immediate, students can receive and apply instantaneous feedback from their teacher, peers, and their own self-reflections that allows them to identify strengths and weaknesses and make needed adjustments in the moment (see figure 5.1).

> "
> *Multiple-choice tests may be easy for machines to mark, but they are of very limited use formatively, with the data offering educators little insight they can use to inform teaching.* (RM Results, n.d., p. 16)

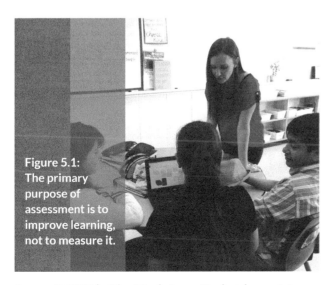

Figure 5.1: The primary purpose of assessment is to improve learning, not to measure it.

Source: © 2017 by Plan Teach Assess. Used with permission.

The subsequent sections examine five components of assessment *for* learning followed by a pair of case studies that illustrate teachers combining these components with assessment through observation and conversation. The chapter concludes with a series of common questions about using a VOCAL approach to improve learning and key messages you should take away from this chapter.

Five Components of Assessment *for* Learning

There is a wealth of research confirming that formative assessment—assessment *for* and *as* learning—is one of the most effective ways to improve student learning (Chappuis & Stiggins, 2020; Moss & Brookhart, 2019; Wiliam, 2018). Paul Black and Dylan Wiliam (2004) argue that the primary purpose of assessment is to improve learning, not to measure it. We believe if every teacher embraces this perspective, they will see dramatically different results in classrooms.

In his research into the power of formative assessment, Wiliam (2011, 2018) identifies five components of assessment *for* learning.

1. **Clarifying learning intentions and sharing criteria for success:** This component stresses the importance of teachers and students having a clear idea about what students must learn during a lesson, unit, or term. Furthermore, students must understand the criteria teachers will use to assess their work, regardless of whether the focus is the acquisition of skills, mastery of content, or creation of products.

2. **Engineering effective discussions, tasks, and activities that elicit evidence of learning:** This component highlights the importance of classroom situations that engage students in effective discussion. When students discuss ideas among themselves (conversations), they explore ideas; reveal misconceptions; listen to and extend one another's thinking; and challenge, encourage, and support one another—all behaviors that ultimately lead students to a deeper understanding of an idea or concept. Whether you, as teacher, are recording the conversation, or one student attached to each group is recording, the result is a rich, reliable, spontaneous record of learning *as it is occurring*!

3. **Providing feedback that moves learners forward:** This component identifies descriptive feedback as the heart of effective formative assessment—effective meaning the feedback leads to improvement. Unfortunately, teacher-written feedback delivered to a student several days after completing a piece of work is of questionable value. Instead, consider feedback delivered face-to-face, in the moment, as a student is performing a task. And if the teacher or another student captures this feedback (either as a recording or typed text on a handheld device), the recipient can listen to it or read it, both immediately and later.

4. **Activating students as learning resources for one another:** This component states students can and must be learning resources for one another. Later in this chapter, you will read about and watch videos of students—both the performers of a task and their peer assessors—collaborating to improve the quality of that task prior to a summative performance for the teacher. Key to this

process is the use of recording devices to both capture the practice performance and the descriptive feedback from the peer assessors.

5. **Activating students as owners of their own learning:** This component points to the need for students to own their learning. The goal of all teaching must be to have students become self-monitoring and self-adjusting learners in order to independently improve the quality of their work. In other words, students must develop metacognitive skills that enable them to think about their own thinking (Cohen et al., 2021). As long as students of any age are dependent on others to tell them whether their work meets a certain standard, they have not truly learned.

Pause and Reflect

- Were you familiar with the components of assessment *for* learning before reading this section?
- As you review the following sections on the five components of assessment *for* learning, consider your current practice relative to each. Identify both areas of current strength and areas for growth.

Assessment *for* Learning in Action

The following sections explore two case studies that reflect the assessment *for* learning components Wiliam (2011, 2018) identifies.

Case Study: Holly Moniz

In Holly Moniz's seventh-grade language arts class, students have just finished reading self-selected novels. They then work in groups, determined by students who selected the same novel to read, to create an infomercial intended to persuade others to read their books. Figure 5.2 illustrates the task outline students received.

Infomercial Project

Purpose: Get your audience to read the book you are trying to sell them.

Your group's task: Create a two-minute infomercial to present live to the class.

Use props, costumes, the Tellagami app, gestures, and enthusiasm to sell your product—your book!

Figure 5.2: Infomercial project outline.

Holly uses the following eight-step process whenever she requires students to demonstrate their learning by working collaboratively to create a significant product.

1. Teacher identifies an authentic task (the infomercial).

2. Teacher and students view exemplars of the task.

3. Teacher and students cocreate success criteria for the task.

4. Teacher and students create a checkbric based on the success criteria.

5. Students present a formative performance of task.

6. Groups, peers, and teacher assess task using checkbric.

7. Groups review feedback and make changes to product or performance.

8. Students present summative performance or submit final product.

Holly introduces how she and her students will cocreate the success criteria for the task by explaining that the work will integrate learning outcomes from the Ontario Ministry of Education (2007b) for reading, oral communication, media literacy, and drama. Students then view a series of commercially available infomercials for themselves to identify the criteria for success. Student groups use Google Drawings to brainstorm sets of success criteria through a teacher-facilitated process, which results in a class consensus. Holly lists the consensus assessment criteria for all students to see (see figure 5.3).

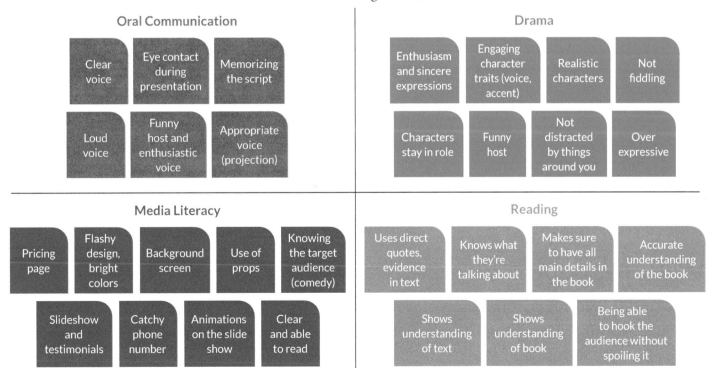

Source: © 2016 by Holly Moniz. Used with permission.

Figure 5.3: Assessment criteria the students and teacher cocreate for the infomercial task.

*Visit **go.SolutionTree.com/assessment** for a free reproducible version of this figure.*

Video 5.1: Teacher and Students Cocreated Success Criteria

Holly facilitates the building of a checkbric based on student-identified success criteria.

Source: © 2017 by Plan Teach Assess. Used with permission.

> *Understanding more about the close relationship between assessment, feedback, and effective learning is the first step toward assessment practices that empower rather than inhibit learning. Technology offers a new perspective through which this relationship can be explored.*
> *(JISC, 2020, p. 19)*

Since this would be an unwieldy assessment tool for students to use, Holly collaborates with her students to transform this set of criteria into a checkbric (see video 5.1). Every student will have the checkbric on his or her own device and use it to assess each of the draft infomercials groups present live.

As you watch video 5.1, consider to what extent this short clip illustrates effective cocreation of assessment criteria by students and teacher. Figure 5.4 shows the completed checkbric students used to formatively assess each group's rough cut of the infomercial.

With a clear set of performance criteria in place, each group spends several class periods creating a first cut of their infomercial. Video 5.2 is an example of one group's first-cut performance. Note that as each group performs their infomercial, their peers in other groups are using the checkbric to assess its strengths and weaknesses.

Video 5.2: A First Cut of a Group Project

A group performs an infomercial project as peers assess its performance using a checkbric.

Source: © 2017 by Plan Teach Assess. Used with permission.

Holly records each group's performance on the numbered tablet assigned to that group (see figure 5.5, page 110). She then hands the performing group its tablet so they can view the recording and begin to make improvements based on the online feedback from their peers, which they review on the group's shared computer (see figure 5.6, page 110).

In video 5.3 (page 110), another group responds to the feedback they received from their peers. Groups also receive direct feedback from Holly, as illustrated in video 5.4 (page 110).

Infomercial Success Criteria Checkbric and Feedback

Please use this cocreated checkbric to provide positive, constructive feedback for the group videos that you are assessing during our peer feedback–loop cycle. Keep one chart per group, and add multiple comments in the boxes provided. If you could use a different color for your feedback than the previous group, that would be awesome! Thanks!

Criteria (Outlined expectations)	Descriptive Feedback (Provide comments.)	En Route (Check off with X.)	Met	Exceeded
Oral communication: Clear and loud voice, eye contact, comfort with the lines, appropriate projection, pace, and speed to ensure audience understanding and engagement	• Memorize the script order	X	X	X
	• Need to practice their lines	X	X	X
	• Good expression	X	X	
	• Very clear and loud voice	X	X	
	• Lots of expression	X	X	
	• Funny and lots of humor			
	• Needs a little less laughing			
	• Needs to be a lot more serious			
Media literacy: Use of media component as a prop, physical props, testimonials as a feature of infomercials, animations within supports, knowing your target audience	• Slideshow supports the infomercial well	X	X	
	• Slide show not that organized			
	• Needs to be organized			
Drama: Engaging host character, staying in role, purposely being over the top	• Funny hosts engaged the audience			X
	• Good acting			X
Reading: Understanding of the text, able to hook the audience with the big ideas without spoiling the book ending, use of direct quotes and evidence	• Understands the book and shows their opinion		X	X
	• Understood the book		X	
Next steps: Memorize lines and practice script. The slideshow needs to be more organized. Improvise with one another, and continue when someone stops or messes up. Add good parts of the book too.				

Source: © 2016 by Holly Moniz. Used with permission.

Figure 5.4: A completed checkbric.

*Visit **go.SolutionTree.com/assessment** for a free reproducible version of this figure.*

Figure 5.5:
Holly recording one group's first cut.

Source: © 2017 by Plan Teach Assess. Used with permission.

Figure 5.6:
A student entering her observations of one of the group's performances.

Source: © 2017 by Plan Teach Assess. Used with permission.

Video 5.3:
Students Discuss Peer Feedback

A student group reviews peer feedback about its first-cut performance.

Source: © 2017 by Plan Teach Assess. Used with permission.

Video 5.4:
Students Receive Teacher Feedback

Holly uses conversation to provide a student group with feedback about its first-cut performance.

Source: © 2017 by Plan Teach Assess. Used with permission.

Once all groups have performed their infomercial first cuts and received online feedback from their peers, Holly coaches students on how to make the best use of the feedback to improve their performances and bring them to camera-ready status (see video 5.5).

Groups then set to work analyzing the online feedback while they review the recording of their performance on the tablet. After groups decide on all the improvements they want to make, they record their infomercial and submit it to Holly for summative assessment. As you consider how you might apply Holly's approach, use the Shift and Share in figure 5.7 (page 112) to support your efforts.

Case Study: Jackie Clarke

In her third-grade class, Jackie Clarke combines her deep understanding of the five components of assessment *for* learning with extensive use of technology to improve students' reading skills. This is a process Jackie replicates with all her students throughout each term.

Jackie's goal is to improve student performance in the core competency of oral reading, something she can't imagine doing without relying on observations of each student's performance alongside one-to-one conversations. To do this, Jackie employs the following eight-step teaching-and-learning cycle to target specific reading fluency skills for each student.

1. Teacher gathers reading assessment data about each student.

2. Student reads orally.

3. Student views video of his or her reading performance.

4. Student sets goals for improvement.

5. Student conferences with a peer coach.

6. Student conferences with the teacher.

7. Teacher communicates with parents.

8. Student meets with parent and teacher.

> *Peer assessment helps learners improve their products by developing a deep understanding of the assessment criteria and their significance, providing opportunities for "learning by example" (Ronen & Langley, 2004) and from classmates' feedback. (Eyal, 2012, p. 42)*

Video 5.5: Teacher Instructions on Using Peer Feedback

Holly coaches students on how to use peer feedback for formative growth.

Source: © 2017 by Plan Teach Assess. Used with permission.

Take a moment to locate yourself on the following teacher-readiness scale. Then reflect on your learning from the preceding case study and decide how you might apply it to your own classroom context. Holly focused on the improvement of a product—a tangible piece of student work—the infomercial. As you choose an application task from the following options, be sure to focus on helping students improve the quality of a product. Of course, a product can take many forms: it can be a written text, a media text, a model, a piece of art, music, a drama, and so on.

	Curiosity "I'm curious to learn about...."	Commitment "I'm taking steps and beginning to...."	Capacity "I'm building on my knowledge and skills for...."	Confirmation "I'm proficient at, and helping others to...."
How do I use balanced assessment to improve learning?	How to use evidence from observations and conversations with students to help them improve their learning	Use evidence from observations and conversations with students to help them improve their learning	Using evidence from observations and conversations with students to help them improve their learning	Use evidence from observations and conversations with students to help them improve their learning

Commitment-Level Application

Review the eight steps Holly used to help students improve the quality of a significant product, in this case, a performance. Examine your current practice relative to the eight steps, and use the following checklist to assess what you are or are not doing in your own practice.

Steps in the Process	Doing	Not Doing
1. Teacher identifies an authentic task.		
2. Teacher and students view exemplars of the task.		
3. Teacher and students cocreate success criteria for the task.		
4. Teacher and students cocreate a checkbric based on the success criteria.		
5. Students perform or create a product that meets task success criteria (formative).		
6. Peers (or peer groups) and teacher use the checkbric to assess the task.		
7. Groups review and reflect on feedback, revising their performance or product.		
8. Students present a final performance or submit a final product (summative).		

Capacity-Level Application

What might this eight-step process look like in your classroom? Identify an authentic product you require students to produce as evidence of their learning. Remember, a product can take many forms: it can be a written or digital text, a piece of art, a music or dramatic performance, a model, and so on. Work through how each of the steps might look in your own classroom.

Confirmation-Level Application

Set up a professional learning session with your colleagues to review and critique the sequence of video clips from Case Study: Holly Moniz (page 106). How might you use this material in your school to help more teachers embrace collecting recorded evidence of learning to improve the quality of student products?

Figure 5.7: Shift and Share—An eight-step process for student products.

*Visit **go.SolutionTree.com/assessment** for a free reproducible version of this figure.*

In video 5.6, Jackie explains her process for engaging in assessment *for* learning with students around oral reading, including her selection of a specific text, *Lost in the Museum* (Cohen, 1996), to support a specific student's needs.

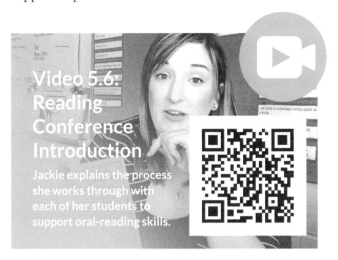

Video 5.6:
Reading
Conference
Introduction

Jackie explains the process she works through with each of her students to support oral-reading skills.

Source: © 2017 by Plan Teach Assess. Used with permission.

Since Jackie's individualized approach to improving reading skills is highly innovative and successful, we have provided extensive transcripts of the videos as a reference for teachers who wish to adopt Jackie's routines:

> The reading response process my students go through is based upon the data I collect early on in the year, whether it's PM [Benchmark] data or the DRA [Developmental Reading Assessment Program] assessment. Using that data, I then decide on the type of book for the instructional level they need for their program. So for Viktoria, she is reading at about a 22, 23, but comprehension is sometimes a little bit lower, so I chose the book *Lost in the Museum* today because it does have some challenging parts for her and is meeting her needs right now, which is working on word parts and chunking. So we worked with that book today, and I just chose the first two pages to kind of give her a little snippet of what the book is about. I recorded her on the iPad and uploaded that to her Halton Cloud (https://sites.google.com/a /hdsb.ca/hdsbcloud) account. Each student has a folder in which they have their videos and then their reading responses. So then the students, and some of them are doing that right now, are watching their videos and watching themselves as a reader. For so many kids, it's the first time they have done that. It's really inspiring and insightful for them to do: "Wow, look what I do. This is incredible" or "Wow, I really need to talk louder." So it's pretty amazing to see the kids do that.
>
> We have come up with, as a class, five questions they need to respond to. They talk about their strengths as a reader, and that is based off of our reading strategies wall. So they are using our CRAFTE strategies to define what they are doing really well as a reader. Then they decide on what are some of my next steps. What are some of the things I need to work on?
>
> Then our class has really been focusing on retelling stories and asking questions. So those are other areas they focus on in their reading response. Once they are finished with their reading response, then they get to have a reading coach. So they meet with another student who has read a completely different story, and they show their reading video and their reading response. Their coach acts like a coach and says to them, "This is something you did really well," or "This is something you could work on."
>
> It's been really good for the kids because it's allowed community building in the classroom, and they really understand this reading continuum. After they have had the opportunity to coach each other, they come to me, and we have a reading conference to talk about what they have done and what their next steps are. So with Viktoria, we came up with a reading bookmark of two things that she needs to work on. At Viktoria's last

conference, we talked about chunking and stopping at periods. And then she uses this bookmark as she reads in the classroom and at home as a constant reminder of, "What are the two things I need to work on?"

After our conference, I send a letter home to the parents to explain what has happened, and the kids love this part because they get to show off their reading to their family. They show their video. They show their conference page with me and their reading response, and then their parents give them feedback. So there's this whole continuous-feedback loop. The kids have watched themselves read five or six times. I just notice their confidence, their reading strategies, and their interest in reading have grown. (Rebooting Assessment, 2021m)

The following sections highlight and explore key aspects of Jackie's approach.

Establishing Learning Goals

The work Jackie does with her students is designed to improve each student's personalized reading goals, which are based on the student's current skill levels and the skills he or she needs to acquire to succeed in the next grade level. She works with each student at the beginning of the process and throughout to set, monitor, and revise goals appropriate to that student. Jackie also sets up the bulletin board (see figure 5.8) to help students set and review these goals. The CRAFTE acronym stands for *comprehension, response to text, accuracy, fluency, text features,* and *expand vocabulary.*

Before continuing, you may wish to refer to the chapter 3 case study featuring Jackie (page 59). It's a useful refresher for how Jackie establishes the classroom routines that enable her to conduct one-to-one reading conferences uninterrupted. Then watch video 5.7 to watch Jackie conference with a student (Viktoria) to review the individual goals Viktoria is working on at that moment. Key to this

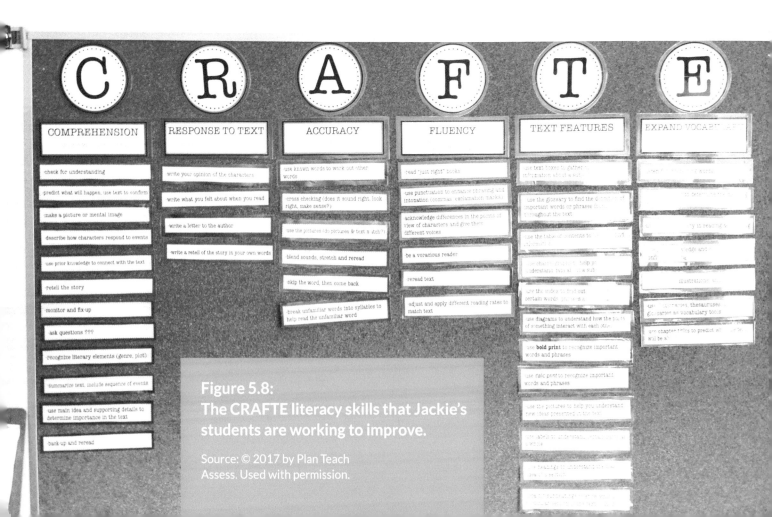

**Figure 5.8:
The CRAFTE literacy skills that Jackie's students are working to improve.**

Source: © 2017 by Plan Teach Assess. Used with permission.

session is the digital recording of Viktoria's reading since it provides the evidence all other steps depend on. We suggest also watching for the following.

- Pay attention to the prereading strategies Jackie uses to prepare Viktoria for her reading performance.

- Notice the behaviors of the rest of the class, visible in the background, during this conference.

Source: © 2017 by Plan Teach Assess. Used with permission.

Notice in the following conversation how Jackie works with Viktoria on prereading strategies:

Jackie: Remember the last time that we met for a conference? We talked about two things we wanted you to work on for next time. Do you remember what those goals were?

Viktoria: Chunking the words and stop at periods.

Jackie: Why do you think it's important for readers to stop at periods?

Viktoria: So that you can like think about the story for what happens and then you can read the next sentence.

Jackie: Right! That kind of breaks up what is going on in the story. And when we are checking words, sometimes we can look for blends like *ch*. Or sometimes we can check words by looking for what? So for like a really big word, what could I do?

Viktoria: You can look at . . . pieces . . . and cut it.

Jackie: Good! So I can cut up the word and find some smaller words inside of it. So today we are starting a new book, and it's called *Lost in the Museum*. Have you ever been to a museum before?

Viktoria: I don't remember.

Jackie: So you are not sure. Well, it's exciting because next week our school will be going to a museum for a field trip. So we are going to be seeing things at the museum. What kind of things do we see at museums?

Viktoria: Like, interesting stuff.

Jackie: Do you know what they call those sometimes? We have been talking about it in social studies.

Viktoria: [Pauses and is unsure what to say]

Jackie: If there is something old and they are being displayed?

Viktoria: [Pauses and is unsure what to say]

Jackie: Artifacts!

Viktoria: Oh, I have never heard that word before.

Jackie: Oh! OK. So this is an artifact on the front cover. [Jackie points at the picture on the cover]. So we are going to be reading *Lost in the Museum*. There are two characters in this book, two little boys. We have Jeff and Tako. And these little boys get themselves into a bit of trouble. (Rebooting Assessment, 2021s)

In the following conversation, Jackie emphasizes for Viktoria how she should carry out her task:

Jackie: So when you are reading, we are going to leave your goals up here. [Jackie places a bookmark with the two goals next to the book.] So you can think about chunking words and stopping at periods. And as you are reading today, I am going to be recording your reading so we can put it into the cloud and you can respond to it. Sound good? So I am going to get the iPad all set up. Today I am going to have you read just these first two pages. [Jackie points to the top of the first page.] You are beginning at chapter 1. This book is broken into chapters so you are going to begin at chapter 1. [Jackie points to the end of the second page.] So you are going to stop here.

There is a bit of a mystery so we are gonna want to know what's going on. [Jackie turns the recording on and places the iPad in a stand next to her on the desk.] And when you are reading I am going to take some notes. [Jackie shows her the notes page.] OK?

Viktoria: Yeah. (Rebooting Assessment, 2021s)

Finally, Viktoria begins reading as Jackie provides necessary scaffolds to support her effort and growth as a reader:

[Viktoria begins to read the story. After a few sentences she pauses at a word. She tries unsuccessfully to pronounce *plaque*.]

Jackie: You can use your strategy by going "pla." So the "que" normally we say "qua." So it's a "pla" "que," plaque.

Viktoria: What does plaque mean?

Jackie: A plaque is something that goes in front of an artifact to tell you what it is. Good question. Why don't you try that sentence again.

[Viktoria continues to read the story.] (Rebooting Assessment, 2021s)

Pause and Reflect

- What prereading strategies did Jackie use to prepare Viktoria for her reading performance?

- What did you notice about the behaviors of the rest of the class, visible in the background, during this conference?

Fundamental to Jackie's approach is, in the words of Wiliam (2018), to "activate students as owners of their own learning" (p. 181). Hence, note that during the initial conference, Jackie recorded Viktoria reading. Following the conference, and with a clear sense of her own individual goals for improvement, Viktoria watches the recording of herself reading (see figure 5.9). She then responds to the following questions.

1. What are your strengths as a reader?

2. What do you need to work on to improve your reading?

3. Retell the story you just read. Include three to six important details.

**Figure 5.9:
Viktoria reviews her
reading performance.**

Source: © 2017 by Plan Teach
Assess. Used with permission.

Providing Feedback That Moves Learners Forward

In video 5.8, Jackie discusses with Viktoria how successful she has been self-critiquing her own reading performance. In this clip and the one to follow, look for evidence that Jackie is doing the following.

- Clarifying learning intentions and sharing criteria for success

- Providing feedback that moves learners forward

- Activating students as the owners of their own learning

Video 5.8: Teacher-Student Follow-Up Interview

Jackie works with a student on her progress in reading.

Source: © 2017 by Plan Teach Assess. Used with permission.

> *Assessment as learning focuses on the role of the student as the critical connector between assessment and their learning. Students, acting as active critical thinkers, make sense of information, relate it to prior knowledge, and use it to construct new learning. This is the regulatory process in metacognition. . . . When teachers focus on assessment as learning, they use classroom assessment as the vehicle for helping students develop and practice the necessary skills to become critical thinkers who are comfortable with reflection and the critical analysis of their learning. (Earl, 2013, p. 28)*

Using anecdotal feedback to clarify what a student is doing well, where problems exist, and how to address those problems is the very essence of assessment *for* learning. In the next step of the learning cycle, Jackie has Viktoria practice her newest strategy on an unfamiliar passage of text (see video 5.9). This is an essential feature of formative assessment since the student is demonstrating how well she is able to apply a newly acquired skill to a previously unseen text.

Source: © 2017 by Plan Teach Assess. Used with permission.

In video 5.9, Jackie and Viktoria have the following conversation around an unfamiliar passage:

Viktoria: See . . . the . . . amazing . . . ex . . . hi . . . bit.

Jackie: So, oh! Strategy time! Let's go back and reread. [Jackie points to the passage] He . . .

Viktoria: He liked riding the bus, eating lunch in the park next to the museum, seeing the amazing exhibit.

Jackie: See how nice that sounds because now it's like I have solved the word, and now I can totally understand what is going on in that sentence. So why don't we try one more time with a sentence we haven't seen before. [Jackie turns the page to a different passage.] Do you want to try that one?

Viktoria: There had been kids and a dog everywhere a minute ago. . . . Oh no, he said everyone has already moved onto the next exhibit. Do you remember where we were . . . sup . . . pose . . .

Jackie: OK. You solved the word; let's go back.

Viktoria: "Do you remember where we were supposed to go next?" asked Jet.

Jackie: How did that feel? Did it feel kind of weird a little bit, or did it feel good?

Viktoria: It felt amazing.

Jackie: It felt amazing! That's awesome. And why did that make you feel so amazing?

Viktoria: Now it makes more sense, and I can understand the story more.

Jackie: That's awesome. That is going to help you understand so well. So I am going to give you this: your new reading strategies card to help you remember when you are reading. And I want you to show this to Mom and Dad. We can either practice or show Mom how your new strategy works. Sound good?

Viktoria: OK. (Rebooting Assessment, 2021e)

Activating Students as Learning Resources for One Another

You've seen throughout *Rebooting Assessment* how learning occurs in social contexts. The renowned Russian psychologist Lev S. Vygotsky (1978) describes the *zone of proximal development* as presenting learners with tasks that challenge but do not frustrate and that the optimum level of challenge presents learners with tasks that are a little more challenging than they could complete alone. You might see this concept expressed in modern contexts as *productive struggle* (Blackburn, 2018) or *desirable difficulty* (Bjork & Bjork, 2014).

Jackie can only conduct one reading conference at a time. So, for meaningful learning to continue after each individual conference, she spends considerable time and effort empowering students to act as peer coaches for one another. Video 5.10 and video 5.11 show Viktoria receiving feedback first from Alexis, her peer coach, alone, and then with some teacher prompting.

To review the success of Jackie's process to this point, consider Viktoria's accomplishments.

- Completed two oral readings while her teacher recorded her performance
- Set goals for improving her reading
- Viewed videos of herself reading
- Critiqued her own reading performance according to these goals
- Met with her peer coach to review and revise her goals on the basis of her most recent reading performance

> *One particularly surprising finding is that the effect of peer tutoring can be almost as strong as one-on-one instruction from a teacher. John Schacter's (2000) study of 109 students in fourth-, fifth-, and sixth-grade classrooms finds that students working in student-led groups learn almost as much as students getting one-on-one tutorial instruction from a teacher, and those in student-led groups actually learn more than those in teacher-led groups. (Wiliam, 2018, p. 157)*

Pause and Reflect

- In your experience, how effective can peer coaching be?
- What are the positives of peer coaching? What are the negatives?
- How can the quality of peer coaching be improved?

Video 5.10: Student Peers Use Conversation to Assess for Learning

Student peers work together to assess a student's progress with reading.

Source: © 2017 by Plan Teach Assess. Used with permission.

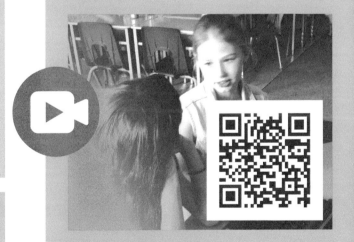

Video 5.11: Teacher Guides Student Peer Coach

Jackie engages in conversations with Viktoria and her peer coach about effective ways to provide formative feedback.

Source: © 2017 by Plan Teach Assess. Used with permission.

It's About Time

Jackie emphasizes that all new approaches to learning take time, including technology-supported approaches to balanced assessment. She further emphasizes the role students play in supporting use of classroom technology:

> *Our students are such technology superstars that we can now use them as supports when using new technology, and they often have fabulous and insightful ideas to make it work! The value in this type of assessment cannot be matched. (J. Clarke, personal communication, September 18, 2016)*

Jackie further explains the benefits of having a quick video to assess as compared to a paper product and how the former empowers students to share their learning in a kaleidoscope of ways, in the moment. Jackie states:

> *A two-minute video is often all you need to plan for next steps! It also brings parents into the conversation about what is happening at school because it allows them to see their child's thinking and learning in action rather than trying to infer and make sense of his or her paper product and our [teachers'] marking. (J. Clarke, personal communication, September 18, 2016)*

Conducting Parent-Student-Teacher Year-End Conferences

The final step in Jackie's process involves a three-way, end-of-year conference that includes Viktoria's mother. This is an opportunity for everyone involved to review Viktoria's progress in reading and identify strategies to employ at home to ensure her reading continues to improve outside school as Viktoria heads into the next grade level. Video 5.12 offers a brief excerpt from the conference.

Video 5.12: Parent-Student-Teacher Conference

Jackie conducts an end-of-year conference with a student and the student's mom.

Source: © 2017 by Plan Teach Assess. Used with permission.

This third-grade case study is a compelling example of the power of the VOCAL approach, coupled with technology-supported video evidence to help a student improve her reading skills. Let's review the process.

- Jackie and Viktoria first agreed on a clear focus for improvement (that is, pausing at periods, and using chunking and rereading to help Viktoria read unfamiliar words).

- Jackie followed a set of eight precise steps with each student to help achieve his or her improvement goals.

- Because the goal is skill development, students, peers, and teachers use descriptive feedback throughout the year to further growth.

- Jackie empowered both Viktoria and Alexis (Viktoria's peer coach) to handle as much of the assessment process as they could. Why? Because student autonomy is essential.

Jackie finds many of her colleagues are skeptical about the time demands of her highly individualized approach to instruction and assessment. But as you can see from the preceding It's About Time section, the biggest obstacle to unlocking this balanced and effective approach to assessment is being willing to tackle the learning curve. To support her colleagues in doing just that, Jackie developed the teacher-planning template in figure 5.10 (page 122) to assist her peers and colleagues in implementing balanced, technology-supported assessments in their classrooms. After taking a moment to reflect on this chart, use the Shift and Share in figure 5.11 (page 123) to assess your readiness to implement a VOCAL approach and your next steps.

Questions About Using the VOCAL Approach to Improve Learning

The following sections address common questions we receive from teachers about using technology to support assessment.

How Do I Manage the Rest of the Class When I'm Working One-on-One With a Student?

As we saw in the Jackie Clarke case study, teachers must invest significant time and energy during the first weeks of a new term to establish class norms regarding behavioral expectations. Then, prior to using an instructional approach in which students are expected to self-monitor time on task and behavior, teachers need to review these expectations. When whole-class instruction resumes, teachers must spend time assessing how well students worked and behaved according to class expectations.

Do I Really Need to Record Students With a Phone or Tablet to Help Them Improve Their Learning?

In both case studies featured in this chapter, Jackie and Holly recorded student performances to facilitate the use of both peer- and teacher-provided descriptive feedback in order to improve learning. The recorded evidence was the focus for all discussions about improvement. In both cases, students reviewed the recordings in light of the feedback they received and were thus able to target specific areas for improvement. While Helen Hills had not employed recorded evidence before our work in her ninth-grade ELA class, she quickly saw the potential benefits after our time with her.

Are All Eight Steps in This Chapter's Case Studies Necessary to Improve Learning?

The eight-step processes Holly and Jackie employ are excellent examples of an instructional cycle that involves the use of diagnostic assessment to identify strengths and needs; targeted, differentiated instruction to address the needs; formative feedback involving teacher, self-, and peer elements; and, finally, summative demonstration of learning leading to grading and reporting. Furthermore, the model draws heavily on the assessment *for* learning research base (Stiggins, 2005; Wiliam, 2018). There isn't a single step among the eight that doesn't serve an essential purpose in using assessment to improve learning. And while this model requires a certain amount of pre-instructional planning and may well represent a significant departure from current practice, it can quickly become a routine for students and teachers alike.

Guiding Questions	Example Look-Fors	Purpose
Planning for learning: • How do you use a backward-design model to plan for student learning? • How do you plan your assessment methods to ensure a balanced approach of observation, conversation, and product evidence? • How do you purposefully plan assessment methods that incorporate technology? • How do you set up your classroom (program and routines) to allow for collection of digital evidence? *For example, if a teacher collects data one-to-one, how do you ensure an environment that allows for collecting this type of evidence?*	• Long-range curriculum plus assessment guide from the school, district, or state or province • Full-day kindergarten learning center plan; school, district, or state or province plan • Secondary school course outline • Classroom cocreated expectations and norms • Classroom tour to show the learning environment	• Model for educators how to use the backward-design planning model. • Model for educators how to plan for assessment to ensure a balanced approach. • Model for educators how to integrate technology into the assessment process and purposefully plan for its implementation. • Model for educators how to structure classroom routines and expectations to allow collection of digital evidence.

Gathering digital evidence:
 	
• What types of digital evidence (conversations or performances) do you choose to record? Why? What is the purpose of recording this evidence? *For example, reading conferences, mathematics congresses, peer feedback on a drama presentation, and so on.*
 	
• What method of technology (*iPad, smartphone, Chromebook*) do you use to collect evidence of conversations and performances?
 	
   ★ Who is doing the recording?
 	
   ★ Where is the digital evidence stored?
	• Recording forms to direct conferences, congresses, feedback sessions, or learning sessions
	
	• Video footage of the collection of digital evidence
		• Model for educators what types of technology to use to collect digital evidence.
		
		• Model for educators the types of assessment data they can capture digitally.
		
		• Model for educators how to capture digital evidence in a classroom setting.

Using digital evidence in the classroom: • How do you use digital recordings for assessment purposes? How does it impact your teaching practice? How does it impact student learning? • Do students interact with the recordings, or are they for teacher use only? If students do see the digital recordings, what is the purpose? *For example, students conference with a teacher or peer, complete a reflection, and so on.* • How do you justify your conversation- and performance-based recordings to students, parents, and administrators? • Do you grade digital recordings? How do you use these recordings as demonstrations of learning?	• Recording forms to direct conferences, congresses, feedback sessions, or learning sessions • Notes and information shared with parents and administrators to justify digital evidence • Rubrics, checklist, and grade book (*paper or digital*) shared plus how to record digital footage as evidence of learning	• Model for educators how to use this type of assessment to make purposeful and data-driven instructions for student learning. • Model for educators how to involve students in the assessment cycle and interact with their own learning and goal setting. • Model for educators how to effectively share digital recordings with students, parents, and the school community.

Source: © 2016 by Jackie Clarke. Used with permission.

Figure 5.10: VOCAL teacher-planning template.

If you currently work at the elementary level, reflect on how Jackie's approach is similar to or different from your own. Are there aspects of Jackie's approach that you could incorporate into your own routines? Review where you see yourself on the teacher-readiness scale, and then select an appropriate application-level task to apply your learning.

	Curiosity "I'm curious to learn about . . . ."	Commitment "I'm taking steps and beginning to . . . ."	Capacity "I'm building on my knowledge and skills for . . . ."	Confirmation "I'm proficient at, and helping others to . . . ."
How do I use balanced assessment to improve learning?	How to use evidence from observations and conversations with students to help them improve their learning	Use evidence from observations and conversations with students to help them improve their learning	Using evidence from observations and conversations with students to help them improve their learning	Use evidence from observations and conversations with students to help them improve their learning

Commitment-Level Application

Review the eight steps Jackie used to help Viktoria improve her oral-reading skills. Use the following checklist to examine your current practice when teaching and assessing essential skills and competencies.

Steps in the Process	Doing	Not Doing
1. Data-gathering regarding the skills (for example, reading assessments)		
2. Student demonstration of skills (for example, oral reading)		
3. Student viewing video of her demonstrating skills (for example, reading performance)		
4. Student setting goals for improvement		
5. Student conference with peer coach		
6. Student conference with teacher		
7. Teacher communicates with parents		
8. Student meeting with parent and teacher to review progress		

Capacity-Level Application

What might this eight-step process look like in your classroom? Choose one essential skill or competency from your own curriculum. It may be from language arts, but it could also be from mathematics or science. Now apply each of the steps to the competency you selected, and decide what it might look like in your own classroom.

Confirmation-Level Application

Set up a professional learning session with your colleagues to review and critique the sequence of case study video clips for Holly and Jackie from this chapter. How might you and your colleagues use this material to help all teachers in your school embrace collecting digital evidence of learning to improve student acquisition of curriculum skills?

Figure 5.11: Shift and Share—Using a VOCAL approach to improve skills or competencies.

*Visit **go.SolutionTree.com/assessment** for a free reproducible version of this figure.*

Key Messages

As you reflect on this chapter, we urge you to focus on the following key messages.

1. When implementing balanced assessment, teachers should aim to emulate the five components of assessment *for* learning (Wiliam, 2011).

    a. Clarifying learning intentions and sharing criteria for success

    b. Engineering effective discussions, tasks, and activities that elicit evidence of learning

    c. Providing feedback that moves learners forward

    d. Activating students as learning resources for one another

    e. Activating students as owners of their own learning

2. Teachers who are successful in using balanced assessment to improve students' learning typically employ a standard set of procedures. For example, in oral reading fluency, a teacher might use the following.

    a. Teacher gathers data.

    b. Student reads orally.

    c. Student views video of his or her reading performance.

    d. Student sets goals for improvement.

    e. Student conferences with a peer coach.

    f. Student conferences with a teacher.

    g. Teacher communicates with parents.

    h. Student meets with parent and teacher.

3. Engaging students fully in critiquing and improving their own learning is an essential component of balanced assessment.

4. Teachers and students using handheld recording devices is a highly effective way to gather and manage assessment evidence.

How Should I Communicate About Learning in the Digital Age?

In this closing chapter, we ask you to think outside the box with respect to how communication about learning needs to change in light of the dramatic shifts in practice that we have examined throughout *Rebooting Assessment*. When students are actively engaged in demonstrating their learning through performance assessment and conversation, while at the same time having their learning journey and their accomplishments captured digitally on smartphones and tablets, does it make sense to rely upon traditional approaches to communication?

In an effort to nudge teachers, administrators, students, and parents toward more effective practice, we propose five significant directions for improving communication about student learning. Several of these directions are already present to some degree in many schools and districts, as the case studies and video clips in this resource demonstrate. Other directions, most notably the fifth, will take longer to implement. But from our point of view, all five represent necessary, positive, and inevitable changes.

1. The traditional push-only method of communicating that focuses on summative data at grade-reporting time will gradually give way to pull communication in which parents, students, and their peers have direct and ongoing access to assessment tasks and criteria, feedback, and information about students' learning.

2. Communication about learning will become increasingly transparent and open, replacing the assessment *black box* (Black & Wiliam, 1998) that Rick Stiggins described as containing a mix of "myth, mystery, and magic" (personal communication, July 13, 2009).

3. Technology will make teaching, learning, and assessment increasingly visible to those outside the classroom.

4. Everyone involved will see students making mistakes as a necessary aspect of learning and growth.

5. Meaningful summaries will replace grades.

> *The current mindset of assessment is all about test scores, irrespective of whether the meaning of the test scores is well clarified. In realising the outcomes of the assessment renaissance, there may not always be a test score to contend with. It may just be a series of qualitative descriptions of the extent to which a student may have demonstrated various attributes that cannot be quantified.* (Hill & Barber, 2014, p. 1)

In this chapter, you will learn more about each of these five directions, which derive naturally from a successful and sustained VOCAL approach to balanced assessment.

Direction 1: *Push* Communication Gives Way to *Pull* Communication

Traditionally, the focus of assessment by educators, students, and parents has been summative, with sights fixated on final percentages or letter grades (Guskey, 2013). Consequently, communication about learning has focused on summative data. When seen this way, assessment is simply an accounting process such that, at predetermined times throughout the school year, teaching and learning stop, replaced with a frenzied scramble to generate grades and comments to fill out report cards (Townsley & Wear, 2020). These grades are then *pushed* out to students and parents as the final, irreversible measure and tally of student learning. Due to the sheer force of generational momentum, these push communications have acquired an almost mythic importance.

One consequence of such infrequent communication to parents is that the first report card often comes as a shock. As I tell teachers in workshops, "Any report card that comes as a surprise to a parent is a bad report card." The problem of the surprise report card is a function of teachers and parents seeing students' grades as the

primary and most important communication about learning. Even in current contexts, where students and parents often have access to grade-reporting systems via an LMS or other platform, the nature of the communications reflects a push-focused mindset. Teachers may not consistently update grade reporting in a timely way, or the system may only allow parents to see summative grades, such as end-of-unit tests. Furthermore, because they are not connected to learning intentions and success criteria, grades are merely crude summaries that don't communicate to students or parents what students know and can do and what they need support with.

Push-focused mindsets to communication are deeply held but reflect seriously flawed views about the primary purpose of assessment. They result from the traditional cycle of teach, test, grade, and move on. So the focus of communication between the teacher and parents has been a student's report card at the end of a term. In this scenario, the report card or online gradebook is the equivalent of an autopsy. From a parent-communication perspective, the reported grades are too little information, coming too late. The learning cycle for a given unit or term is over, and the grades are merely cause for celebration or recrimination.

Going forward, communication about learning needs to involve, at the very least, a balance of pull and push communication. To extend the metaphor, what students and parents need to receive *during* the learning process is a *prescription*, not an *autopsy* (Cooper, 2016; DuFour et al., 2016). When there is time to improve learning *before* grades are determined, each student needs a specific prescription detailing actions he or she needs to take to improve. And parents need to see where their child is on a learning progression, both to know whether sufficient progress is being made and to support learning at home (see figure 6.1).

The prevalence of handheld digital technology and high-quality software, such as an LMS and other platforms with online gradebooks that also facilitate communication between all stakeholders, means teachers can keep parents in the loop about their child's learning as it is occurring in the classroom. When used to support a balanced approach to assessment, such platforms routinely push in-the-moment updates to parents about work their children are doing at school via smartphone and tablet apps that provide easy access to communications (see figure 6.2). These updates may include artifacts, a video of an oral reading, a demonstration of science skills, a musical performance, a basketball drill, or a conversation in French, to name just a few examples.

The trick with these platforms is the aforementioned need for balance. If platforms are too convoluted for parents to easily access, many won't. Similarly, and as noted earlier in this section, if teachers don't keep online reports up to date, even parents who check in on their child's progress may not receive information they can act on until it's too late. And if the platforms focus only on grade notifications that are disconnected from actual student work, such reports remain autopsies rather than prescriptions.

On the other end of the spectrum, parents may find 24-7 access and updates more of a curse than a blessing. Most parents appreciate being informed, but constant and unnecessary text or email notifications can be annoying and result in parents tuning out such messages. So here are some guidelines that will help teachers and students ensure that ongoing communications to parents are welcome.

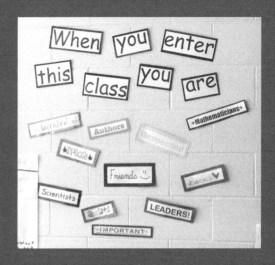

Figure 6.1:
Pull communications take parents inside the classroom.

Source: © 2016 by Jackie Clarke. Used with permission.

Submitted Student Product or Recording

Teacher Comments With Feedback

Figure 6.2:
An LMS can provide parents with in-the-moment updates about learning.

Teacher communication to parents includes the preceding, plus information about:

- Learning outcomes
- Self-reflection from the student about their work
- Descriptive teacher feedback that includes an evaluative component
- Next steps in the learning journey

1. Most parents want to know the broad, essential learning goals their child is working on. For students in the primary grades (K–2), these goals may relate to a student's progress along a learning continuum relating to, for example, literacy, numeracy, or social skills (see figure 6.3).

2. Parents also want to know the major sources of evidence—conversations, performances, projects, presentations, products—the teacher will use to assess if each student has met the broad learning goals.

3. While many parents may not understand their importance, teachers should communicate the criteria by which these major pieces of work will be assessed. This is vital so parents clearly understand which aspects of an assessment are essential and which are not. For example, the British Columbia's (BC's) Curriculum (https://curriculum.gov.bc.ca) includes criteria that relate to learning standards using *I can* statements, a useful way

to express criteria using student- and parent-friendly language. They use the statements (on the site's Profiles tab), such as the following criteria that relate to critical thinking and reflective thinking (BC's Curriculum, n.d.):

> I can explore.
>
> I can use evidence to make simple judgments.
>
> I can ask questions and consider options. I can use my observations, experience, and imagination to draw conclusions and make judgments.
>
> I can gather and combine new evidence with what I already know to develop reasoned conclusions, judgments, or plans.
>
> I can evaluate and use well-chosen evidence to develop interpretations; identify alternatives, perspectives, and implications; and make judgments. I can examine and adjust my thinking.
>
> I can examine evidence from various perspectives to analyze and make well-supported judgments about and interpretations of complex issues.

Typical Skill Acquisition for Students in Grade 1

Grade 1: First Term	Grade 1: Second Term	Grade 1: Third Term

Grade 1: First Term	Grade 1: Second Term	Grade 1: Third Term
Picture matches writing Text tends to be in random order	Picture shows some events Shows list-like sequence of events or details • Evidence of a beginning • Uses some basic transitions (*next, then*) correctly Links sentence parts (*and, so*)	Picture reflects essence of text Most sentences are in sequential order and connected. • Beginning reflects main idea; evidence of an ending • Uses most basic transitions (*next, then*) correctly • Most parts fit and make sense. Links sentence parts (*and, so, because*) Title states topic

Source: Adapted from Cooper, 2011.

Figure 6.3: A partial sample growth continuum for grade 1 writing.

4. Parents will benefit from frequent updates about their child's progress on the learning goals or their growth relative to the learning continua.

5. Parents will appreciate receiving updates from both their child and the teacher. From the child, the update may be an image, a video clip, or an artifact, along with a "Look what I just did!" message. From the teacher, the update may be a more specific communication about how the student's work provides evidence of progress toward one of the essential learning goals.

These guidelines suggest a common theme: all digital data teachers and students make available to parents should provide useful information about some aspect of students' learning. In educational circles, we like to use the term *evidence* to help clarify the essential connection between teaching and learning (Wiggins & McTighe, 2005). In a process that involves matching provincial or state curricula with individual students or groups of students in their class, teachers develop instructional plans that aim to move students from their current level of knowledge and skills to the next stage in their learning. In a VOCAL approach, assessment involves gathering evidence as this learning occurs and then sharing it with students and parents to help the former improve their learning and to help the latter understand how well their child is progressing. The term *evidence* helps everyone involved—teachers, students, and parents—understand that the shared information is relevant to the learning goals.

Direction 2: Communication About Learning Becomes Open and Transparent

A feature and benefit of pull communication are how it naturally leads to greater transparency and openness in the assessment process. Education is personal for teachers, students, and parents. And because everyone involved brings different perspectives, experiences, and

It's About Time

We often hear the question: "Where do I find the time to have all these communications with parents?" Guidelines 1, 2, and 3 all involve teachers doing some initial work. But once teachers create documents for a given year's program or course, they can reuse those documents repeatedly. Frequent updates are then specific to each student (guidelines 4 and 5). But as we explain throughout *Rebooting Assessment*, students can and should curate much of this information. From a teacher perspective, the VOCAL approach involves far less time spent during the panic before each reporting period and marking written work outside of class time. Instead, more time is spent in the moment, observing and listening to students and sharing a sample of the regularly gathered digital evidence. As Holly Moniz (see her case study, page 106) explains, "It's not about adding more time, but reallocating time" (personal communication, October 22, 2016).

expectations to the table, teachers' willingness to reveal their vulnerability and emotional response to the challenges of teaching, learning, and assessment can establish a foundation for deeper and more productive engagement—for all.

When reflecting on traditional approaches to communicating with students and parents about assessment, I often think of my own experiences. For example, as a parent, I remember well attending a parents' night when my son, Chris, was in ninth grade. Chris had excelled in ELA throughout his elementary school years, yet his November report card grade was in the 60 percent range. Puzzled about this sudden drop, I inquired of his teacher, "Could you tell me how you determined Chris's grade?" I expected her to produce her gradebook in answer to my question. Instead, she hesitated for a moment and said, "Now let me see. They did a group newspaper. . . . And then there was a group seminar. . . ." At this point, I interjected, "Tell me what individual pieces of work contributed to Chris's grade." She informed me there had been none during the first term.

Clearly, this anecdote raises a number of troubling issues, including the problem of group grades. But for purposes of transparency, this example serves to illustrate the opaque nature of push-only communication, with teacher-initiated reporting exclusively at the end of grading periods. Until Chris's report card arrived on my kitchen table, I had no idea of what was going on in his class. And yes, his report card grade came as a shock when compared with his consistent performance in ELA throughout his previous years of schooling.

Contrast this situation with the ongoing, frequent, and transparent communication about learning that characterizes Jackie Clarke's approach in chapter 5 (see Case Study: Jackie Clarke, page 111). Jackie makes extensive use of video recording of the students in her third-grade reading program at every stage of the assessment, teaching, and learning processes (see figure 6.4).

Figure 6.4: Jackie working with Viktoria.

Source: © 2017 by Plan Teach Assess. Used with permission.

Specifically, Jackie does the following.

- Uses video diagnostically to help determine each student's reading level in September, as well as to assist in setting goals for improvement

- Immediately uploads videos to each student's online account so they are accessible to students, parents, and teachers at any time

- Records each subsequent reading conference with each student to chart his or her improvement

- Assigns students to self-assess their recordings

- Conducts three-way conferences between herself, students, and parents periodically throughout the year to discuss and demonstrate each student's areas of progress and needed improvement

In this way, the parents of Jackie's students have access to evidence of their child's learning at any time via Jackie's cloud-based approach. They can also count on regular meetings with their child and Jackie to provide specific information about learning. This is what transparent and open communication looks like.

Direction 3: Technology Makes Teaching, Learning, and Assessment More Visible

As an educator, I have always believed assessment is not something teachers do *to* students. At its best, *assessment* is a collaborative process that engages the students, teachers, and parents in the pursuit of learning. Fortunately, schools that embrace a balance of push and pull communication, as well as transparency in the assessment process and the use of digital technology to capture evidence of learning, find that students and parents become increasingly engaged and involved. This enhanced involvement, in turn, expands opportunities for teachers to engage students and parents in the vital role of assessment *as* learning (Earl, 2013). This requires students to take greater responsibility for monitoring and improving their own learning. Meanwhile, as parents become more comfortable and adept with using online gradebook portals and accessing ePortfolios, they enhance their ability to be partners in their child's learning.

Pause and Reflect

- How involved are the parents of your students in their children's learning?
- Would greater parent involvement benefit their children's learning?

Increased transparency in communication that leads to more parent involvement makes the work teachers do more visible. Teaching and learning becoming more visible to those outside the classroom have both benefits and drawbacks. When I was a child, my parents would not have dreamed of questioning my teachers about the decisions they made at school, in part because what went on

in the classroom was invisible to them. Teachers were considered experts in their chosen field, and communication was essentially one way—teachers sent home periodic summaries in the form of grades. Even parent interviews were largely one-way communications that only occurred once or twice during the school year. Any call to meet with a teacher outside of that framework implied some kind of bad news.

How things have changed! Many teachers we have worked with during the past decade live in constant fear of parents challenging them over their decisions. Parents are more likely to side with their child rather than with the teacher when questions arise. Consider, however, that this sort of friction often occurs precisely because teaching and learning aren't truly visible. When communication about learning is both *pull* and transparent, and when student work is readily available and paired with student- and parent-friendly learning intentions and success criteria, the purpose and process of learning become clearer. As a result, questions between teachers and parents focus on that process and how to best support learning, especially regarding assessment (see figure 6.5). Making teaching and learning visible has been a popular theme in research (Hattie, 2009, 2012; Hattie & Clarke, 2019).

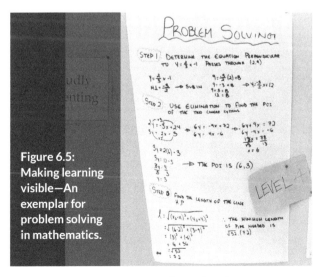

Figure 6.5: Making learning visible—An exemplar for problem solving in mathematics.

Source: © 2016 by Jamie Mitchell. Used with permission.

From a negative perspective, as a result of this greater scrutiny, many teachers we meet are becoming less confident of their craft. "Am I allowed to do that?" has become a frequent refrain in our sessions with educators. Left unchecked, this lack of confidence can undermine teachers' professionalism. Teachers, like other professionals, must see themselves as *lifelong learners*. Some may regard this term as tired and overused, but it is vitally important. In no other profession would practitioners consider it acceptable *not* to keep abreast of current research. In the words of researcher and author John Hattie (2012), "Know thy impact" (p. ix). He advises teachers to see their classrooms as research laboratories; every day, they must ask, "What impact did I have on my students today? Were there students I did not impact? Why? What might I have done differently?" These are research questions, and given the nature of their work, teachers have the opportunity, every day, to conduct experimental research to answer them. Such *action research*, conducted informally by teachers, simply means making a change to your practice that you believe will improve learning, collecting data about whether that change was effective, and then adjusting your approach based on those findings (Kolk, n.d.).

Making assessment more visible to parents has been a welcome trend as schools increasingly adopt standards-based grading practices. The shift from norm-referenced to criterion-referenced grading practices is an impetus for greater transparency in classroom assessment (Cooper, 2011; Guskey, 2015; O'Connor, 2018). Teachers providing—and parents demanding!—rubrics to accompany assigned tasks are a clear reflection of this trend. I am embarrassed to recall the early years of my high school English teaching career. It was common practice for me to assign a major piece of writing to students, have them complete the work, and then collect the papers, take them home, and ask myself, "Now what was I looking for on this task?" By contrast, the majority

of high school English teachers I encounter in my work routinely do the following.

- Examine models and exemplars of the intended learning or task with students.

- Collaborate with students to identify assessment criteria by which the work will be assessed.

- Develop a student-friendly rubric based on the criteria.

- Use a process model that monitors students' understanding as they engage with the learning or task.

- Provide formative feedback on early drafts or attempts, using the rubric.

- Assess the learning or task and provide feedback via the rubric.

It has been common practice in high schools to rank students based on numerical scores—87 percent is just slightly above 86 percent (see figure 6.6). But this thinking reflects *norm-referenced grading*, which compares students one against another. If, on the other hand, teachers' focus is observing what students can do and listening to how well they understand when engaged directly in authentic assessment tasks, then the grading process involves certifying their level of proficiency against a public standard such as a shared rubric written in student and parent-friendly language. In other words, the grading process becomes both criterion referenced and visible. Far from ranking students one against another with no clear performance standards, *criterion-referenced grading* requires the teacher to make informed professional judgments by comparing each student's performance to a well-defined and visible scale based on what students must actually know and be able to do (see figure 6.7, page 136).

Norm-referenced grading also fosters a lack of transparency and visibility in traditional reporting methods and formats. Not surprising when the reference point for grading is the sliding scale of how the rest of the class performs! So students and parents receive summarized omnibus (overall) grades, such as 81 percent. But what, precisely, does such a grade mean? Summary grades obscure whatever learning may have occurred. In no other human endeavor would we be so foolish as to quantify proficiency using a 100-point scale. Just what does 83 percent driving look like?

For now, since we seem to be stuck with percentages, the best question that a student or parent can ask is: "What does 81 percent in English mean?" This compels the teacher to disaggregate the summary grade into more meaningful information. For example, consider Greg, who received a grade of 81 percent on his report card for ELA. Unlike my son's teacher, mentioned earlier, one would hope that the teacher in this case would access her gradebook, or perhaps the student's portfolio, to reveal that the summary grade breaks down into more specific information, such as the following.

- Oral communication: 90 percent
- Reading and literature: 85 percent
- Writing: 65 percent
- Media studies: 85 percent

In this case, parents gain some modicum of insight into the learning behind Greg's 81 percent. Greg and his parents can see that he has demonstrated less proficiency in written communication than in the three other strands. From that information, the teacher, Greg, and his parents can focus attention on improvement in the writing strand (see figure 6.8, page 137).

However, even in this example, the teacher is still using *quantitative* measures for skills that are *qualitative* in nature (Cooper, 2010). This is where the VOCAL approach shines. With captured evidence of what students know and can do, expressed through conversations and performances, a teacher can now say, "Let's watch a brief video that illustrates Greg's proficiency with *reading for meaning*." By using technology to make what Greg read visible, both he and his parents can see

> "
>
> *Recognizing excellence in academic performance is a vital aspect of any learning community. But such recognition need not be grounded on norm-based criteria that lead to deleterious competition. Instead, it should be based on clear models of excellence.... Educators concerned more with developing talent than with selecting talent should take pride in helping the largest number of students possible meet the rigorous criteria and high standards of excellence.* (Guskey, 2015, p. 69)

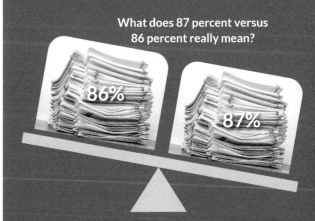

What does 87 percent versus 86 percent really mean?

Source: © 2017 by Plan Teach Assess. Used with permission.

Figure 6.6: Norm-referenced grading compares students' performance to one another based on numerical scores.

Achievement standards

Source: © 2017 by Plan Teach Assess. Used with permission.

Figure 6.7: Criterion-referenced grading compares student performance to a public standard.

> If someone proposed combining measures of height, weight, diet, and exercise into a single number or mark to represent a person's physical condition, we would consider it laughable. . . . Yet every day, teachers combine equally diverse measures of students' performance in school into a hodgepodge grade that is just as confounded and impossible to interpret as a physical condition grade that combined height, weight, diet, and exercise—and no one questions it. (Guskey, 2011)

evidence conveyed through context and meaning of what skills and knowledge Greg has mastered and where he still has room for improvement. That said, I would challenge any teacher's ability to explain to a parent the difference between an 85 percent demonstration of a skill and an 84 percent or 83 percent demonstration of that skill! I'm sorry, but the emperor has no clothes!

Direction 4: Mistakes and Flaws Are Seen as Essential to Learning and Growth

My observations from the previous section that most high school English teachers I encounter provide formative feedback on early student drafts using a rubric points to an important fourth direction. That is the normalization and acceptance of students making mistakes as they develop skills, the acceptance of flaws in new learning, and an openness to what is not going well as necessary aspects of improvement (see figure 6.9). You have seen this referred to in this book as *productive struggle* (Blackburn, 2018; Grafwallner, 2021).

When learning is new and unfamiliar, teachers must *expect* students to get things wrong; they should expect a flawed demonstration of new learning. The teacher, acting as coach and facilitator, then focuses or differentiates instruction to address the specific nature of an individual student's struggle (or the struggles of a small group of students facing the same challenge).

Unfortunately, in many elementary classrooms we visit, teachers and students have an aversion to errors. Too often, a culture of "awesomeness" prevails. I would like to impose a moratorium on the use of the word *awesome*. Teachers often toss it out like Halloween candy, but it's a summative

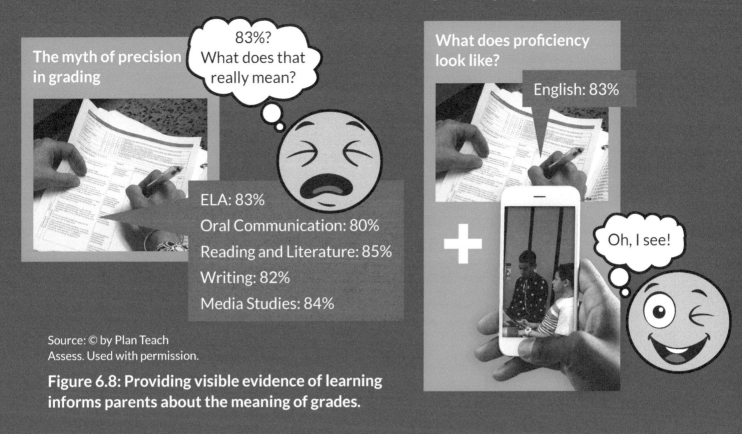

Source: © by Plan Teach Assess. Used with permission.

Figure 6.8: Providing visible evidence of learning informs parents about the meaning of grades.

word teachers should reserve for polished work worthy of this description. It's *not* a word teachers should use to motivate further effort. Often, teachers use this and similar words as a misapplication of research concerning a growth mindset. It is crucial that teachers distinguish between effort and proficiency. A student may be commended for demonstrating hard work, but that must not be viewed as a substitute for demonstrated proficiency. Furthermore, prematurely telling students their work is "awesome" is more likely to lead to a cessation of effort rather than to an increase (Dweck, 2016).

Based on my own teaching experience when working with students who have severe learning disabilities, *a child's improved self-esteem never derives from a false sense of achievement* (Cooper, 2011). Teachers, students, and parents all need to see learning as challenging, messy, and fraught with early failure. As educators, none of us should seek to conceal mistakes when learning is tentative, skills are imperfect, and misconceptions are common. Getting

things wrong initially provides teachers with the raw material they need to instruct effectively.

And so communication about learning *during* the instructional process should include honest, accurate information about errors, mistakes, and misconceptions, not superficial, misleading descriptions of work as being "awesome." As we

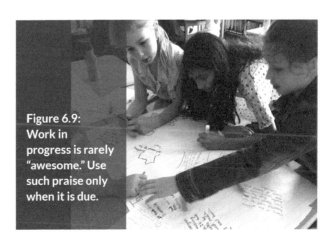

Figure 6.9: Work in progress is rarely "awesome." Use such praise only when it is due.

Source: © 2017 by Plan Teach Assess. Used with permission.

have seen, transparent communication that makes learning visible to parents enables them to see in-the-moment digital evidence of their child's work in progress. Typically, this will reveal unsuccessful early tries, errors in thinking and procedures, misconceptions, undeveloped skills, and so on. All these provide teachers with information they need to adjust instruction through targeted intervention and students with information to change, revise, or modify their approach.

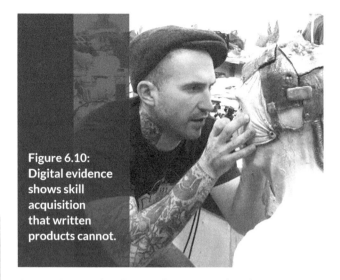

Figure 6.10: Digital evidence shows skill acquisition that written products cannot.

Source: © 2017 by Plan Teach Assess. Used with permission.

> ## Pause and Reflect
>
> - What is your reaction to the statement, "A child's improved self-esteem never derives from a false sense of achievement"?
>
> - Do you notice yourself or your colleagues meting out praise too frequently, especially when work is not *awesome*?

Direction 5: Grades Are Replaced by Meaningful Summaries of Learning

When my son, Chris, secured a job with a movie and TV special effects company in 2011, I said to him, "I guess your good grades in college got you the job, right?" "Sure, Dad," Chris replied sarcastically before saying, "This is what got me the job!" Chris held up his smartphone to show me his ePortfolio, which included videos of zombie makeup jobs and pictures of gruesome prosthetic body parts he'd created (see figure 6.10).

Many schools already use ePortfolios to store digital evidence of students' learning, and if they can do that, they can also use a selected sample of this evidence for grading and reporting to parents. Yet, when we examine reporting formats across North America—and indeed around the world—we see little change from traditional 20th century practices. With a few notable exceptions, we see countless spreadsheets with lots of numerical data but very little useful information about students' learning.

End-of-term report cards that highlight numerical or letter grades over meaningful, qualitative information about student learning are consistent with the view of assessment as a process of quantifying learning. Stiggins (1994) connects this view of assessment with the United States' preoccupation with standardized testing, beginning in the 1920s and into the 1990s. Unfortunately, the educational assessment community, from the primary grades through postsecondary, continues to be obsessed with *quantifying learning*, a reciprocal process in which the more educators provide students and parents with numerical scores, the more students and parents demand them, even if those numbers are insufficient to support actual learning and engagement in productive struggle.

Is this craving for scores innate? No, it is taught and learned, beginning in the earliest grades at school. In numerous workshops over the years, I have asked the question, "At what grade level do students begin to ask questions such as, 'What did I get?' and 'Does this count?'" The vast majority of teachers answer third grade; however, it's common to hear first grade too. And so the *cult of measurement* (Cody & Bower, 2013) becomes deeply ingrained in students' minds at a formative age. As students progress from grade to grade, the use of *proxy instruments* (products) to measure learning—tests, examinations, term papers—increases, deepening the conviction that teachers must use numerical scores to describe and summarize learning (see figure 6.11).

Unfortunately, because the *quantification* of learning is so deeply ingrained in assessment practice, all stakeholders— educators, students, and their parents—expect, if not demand, scores, even when *qualitative* information would be far more useful and desirable. In earlier chapters, we focused on how teachers can and should make use of rich digital data captured through conversations and performances for the purpose of improving learning. Even when the assessment purpose is summative, and the only time when grades—numerical, letter, or rubric level—are appropriate, we also advocate for teachers to accompany

> *Change leaders of successful grading policies embrace a clear set of principles about the fundamental purposes of grading as a tool for improved student learning. They reject grading as a form of punishment and manipulation and embrace it as a means of communication and feedback. Their purpose is neither to sort students nor to judge them but to help them become more successful. (Reeves, 2016, p. 154)*

Figure 6.11: Teaching third-grade about the benefits of intrinsic rewards.

Source: © 2017 by Plan Teach Assess. Used with permission.

those summative grades, wherever possible, with digital evidence of learning.

> ❝
> **There is an expectation that assessment culminates in a score but could society live with qualitative statements for skills/attributes that cannot easily be quantified?** (RM Results, n.d., p. 26)

Set aside your educator hat for a moment, and assume the role of parent. Let's say your daughter, Emma, is in second grade. You've just received her second-term report card; figure 6.12 illustrates the *Reading* portion. How much useful, meaningful information do the letter grades and accompanying comment communicate?

Now, consider an alternative rooted in technology-supported balanced assessment with a focus on pull communication. Instead of a final report card and a brief, low-impact comment acting as feedback, you receive on your phone a series of short video clips occurring at intervals throughout the first and second terms as pictured in figure 6.13, along with access to a chart for reading-skills growth. How might this expanded version impact your understanding of Emma's actual improvement over time?

Throughout *Rebooting Assessment*, you have seen the power of technology-supported balanced assessment this example represents. But we recognize teachers and even schools typically do not have full control over the structure and format of end-of-term and end-of-year reporting. That does not prevent you, as a teacher, from augmenting that reporting with this kind of evidence. Consider how you can

enter a transitional stage in your own practice; parents receive *both* a traditional report card and visual recorded evidence, such as figure 6.13 shows.

What Grades Should Measure

In the previous section, we talked about Emma's progress in reading, but what does a *B* in the first term and an *A* in the second term actually mean? To answer this question, it helps to think back to chapter 1's (page 12) differentiation of *growth*, *progress*, and *achievement* as three distinctly different ways to measure students' learning (see figure 6.14, page 142). It follows that teachers' communication and reporting processes must align perfectly with their assessment processes.

Does Emma's reading grade of a *B* mean that her ability to read has *grown* according to where she started? Does it refer to the amount of *progress* she made in improving her reading skills in each term? Or, does it mean that she *achieved* B-quality reading in the first term and A-quality reading in the second term?

Holly works hard with both her students and their parents to maintain a focus on learning rather than grading. In addition to the videos for her case study in chapter 5 (page 104), in video 6.1 (page 142), she explains how communicating about progress through anecdotal information enables her to provide meaningful measures of student learning.

Student: Emma Davis			Grade: 2
Subject	Report Period		Strengths and Next Steps for Improvement
	1	2	
Language (reading)	B	A	Emma has shown significant improvement in her reading since the first term.
☐ English language learner			
☐ Individualized education program			

Source: © 2017 by Plan Teach Assess. Used with permission.

Figure 6.12: A traditional report card entry provides very little useful information to parents.

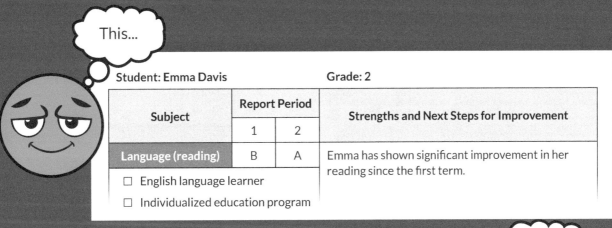

Figure 6.13 content: Thought bubble "This..."

Student: Emma Davis			Grade: 2
Subject	Report Period		Strengths and Next Steps for Improvement
	1	2	
Language (reading)	B	A	Emma has shown significant improvement in her reading since the first term.
☐ English language learner			
☐ Individualized education program			

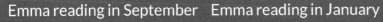

Emma reading in September   Emma reading in January   Emma reading in June

Source: © 2017 by Plan Teach Assess. Used with permission.

Figure 6.13: Digital evidence of a student's improvement over time.

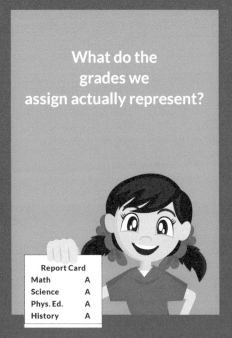

What do the grades we assign actually represent?

Growth
A measure of the increase of student learning over time, but with no specific performance target in mind

Progress
A measure of student learning over time, toward an expected standard

Achievement
A snapshot of student learning at a moment in time

Source: © 2017 by Plan Teach Assess. Used with permission.

Figure 6.14: Three distinct ways to grade learning.

Video 6.1: Teacher Interview on Learning, Growth, and the Report Card

Holly explains how she communicates student progress.

Source: © 2017 by Plan Teach Assess. Used with permission.

Notice in video 6.1 how Holly explains her school's use of progress reports and how they are particularly beneficial early in the school year as a way to provide formative feedback when it's most impactful, reserving ministry (summative) report cards for much later in the school year (February and June). She states:

I find that helps the beginning of the year really set up because when we have our parent lead conferences and parents are coming in to us and having discussions, they [students] still haven't received a formal grade on their report cards yet. Often what they are receiving in class is feedback. And although they have different rubrics and different checkbrics, different success criteria, tools, whatever we're using, they're gathering that information and using it to formulate their understanding about growth. It's about the learning. It's about getting kids to realize how we can get them to be the best possible version of themselves and having the parents on board with that.... The conversations are really about improvement and about what students can do to enhance their performance in all subject areas. (Rebooting Assessment, 2021dd)

Educators must be mindful of the significant differences between growth, progress, and achievement when assessing learning and when reporting on that learning (see figure 6.15). In the primary grades, or when students enter school from another country and are not fluent in the native language of their adoptive country, measuring growth is appropriate and desirable. As students become more proficient, it may be appropriate to shift to a measure of progress toward established benchmarks to ensure learning is on track relative to age and grade-level expectations. Measuring achievement is often necessary and appropriate when determining a student's prior learning for purposes of entry into a specific course of study or to certify a required level of proficiency for credentialing.

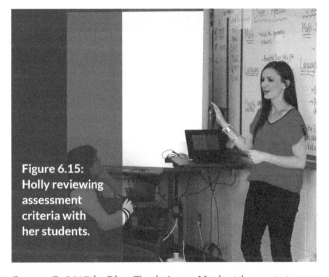

Figure 6.15: Holly reviewing assessment criteria with her students.

Source: © 2017 by Plan Teach Assess. Used with permission.

I have long been an advocate for providing parents with grades that communicate information about both achievement and progress (Cooper, 2011). Unfortunately, too often at the secondary level, grading procedures based solely on achievement result in teachers communicating the wrong messages about learning. Think of a student who earns an *A* in each term while putting forth little or no effort. On the other end of the spectrum is a student who fails the first term but works extremely hard to achieve a *C* in the next term, still not shaking the label of *low achiever*. While the

C conveys that there is still more ground for the latter student to cover, the letter grade as an isolated summary of achievement does not communicate the significant progress this student made.

With some notable exceptions, most report cards fail to make clear whether they are communicating information about growth, progress, achievement, or some combination of the three. This is easily remedied by providing a simple explanatory key for parents on the document. The greater challenge is ensuring that all teachers are, themselves, clear about whether they are assessing and reporting on growth, progress, or achievement!

We strongly believe that in this digital age, teachers have at their disposal powerful tools to communicate with parents far more effective summaries of their children's learning than traditional reporting formats provide (see figure 6.16, page 144).

To further support these efforts, consider how the ePortfolio systems we discussed in chapter 4 (page 74) can act as both powerful assessment tools and highly effective vehicles for reporting. This is especially true in the hands of a teacher like Jackie (see video 6.2).

Video 6.2: Three-Way Conference Between Teacher, Student, and Parent

Jackie conferences with a student and her mother.

Source: © 2017 by Plan Teach Assess. Used with permission.

During the conference, Jackie explains to student Viktoria's mother how much progress Viktoria made that year. They review short video clips of Viktoria

**Figure 6.16:
A three-way conference.**

Source: © 2017 by Plan Teach
Assess. Used with permission.

reading in September, November, and February. Then, Viktoria reads aloud, "live." Jackie explains to Viktoria's mother the specific reading skills she has improved by referring to the classroom's Reading Strategies Wall. This kind of live reporting is exactly what we advocate: capture and share visual and oral evidence of students' developing proficiency with respect to essential learning targets. After all, at the end of a term, a grading and reporting system should inform parents about how much improvement their child has demonstrated and whether that improvement is sufficient according to grade-level expectations.

How to Convince Parents About the Value of Digital Evidence of Learning

Schools and teachers cannot and should not expect to dictate the degree to which parents become partners in their child's learning. What educators can do is ensure parents can avail themselves of the information they need and want. In that regard, put on your parent hat and consider whether these are the questions you would want a teacher to answer about your child's learning.

Pause and Reflect

- Review the definitions for *growth*, *progress*, and *achievement* in chapter 1 (page 12). Which of these measures are you currently grading and reporting to parents?

- How collaborative are your current communication processes in involving students and their parents?

- What are the most important things my child is learning this year or in this course?

- What evidence should I expect to see from my child that demonstrates this learning?

- Against what measure or scale are you assessing my child's work?

- Is my child progressing as you expect, relative to this scale?

- How can I support my child's learning at home?

Notice that these very same questions gave rise to the guidelines for communicating with parents we introduced as part of push and pull communication earlier in this chapter. You may wish to review our recommendations there as to how to respond to the questions.

But as we have stressed throughout this resource, providing parents with visible evidence of their child's learning by activating the power of digital technology holds great potential for engaging them deeply. When parents actually see video evidence of their child playing a musical instrument, speaking French, conducting a science experiment, or sharing personal reflections with classmates, they come to understand the shortcomings of traditional pencil-and-paper assessments.

Sharing the benefits of visible evidence of learning with parents is essential if teachers are to move away from a systemic overreliance on standardized, written testing that has traditionally overemphasized knowledge recall. Instead, educators need to move toward a pedagogically sound and balanced view of assessment that acknowledges a wide range of learning goals and focuses on the whole student.

Perhaps the biggest challenge is to convince the adults involved that digital evidence of learning is as valid as more traditional forms of summative assessment when it comes to making grading and reporting decisions (see figure 6.17). Our experience suggests the students are already on board!

Source: © 2017 by Plan Teach Assess. Used with permission.

Figure 6.17: The challenge of parent buy-in about balanced assessment.

Our advice, once again, is to step outside the classroom and ask parents to consider examples from their own experience. For example, ask:

- "Would you want to share the road with young drivers who had been certified as proficient purely on the basis of their scores on the standardized written test based on the driver's handbook?"

- "Would you patronize a conservatory of music that prided itself on evaluating its pupils' music performance skills using only written examinations?"

- "Can you imagine a modern professional sports franchise winning a national championship without making extensive use of recordings of games played during the regular season?"

Having used these arguments myself in discussions with numerous parents, I can assure you of their power to convince. As you consider your own approach to this important task, use the Shift and Share in figure 6.18 (page XX) to assess your position on the teacher-readiness scale.

Review the following section of the teacher-readiness scale. Where would you put yourself on the scale? Based on your comfort level, select an application task from the choices that follow.

	Curiosity "I'm curious to learn about . . . ."	Commitment "I'm taking steps and beginning to . . . ."	Capacity "I'm building on my knowledge and skills for . . . ."	Confirmation "I'm proficient at, and helping others to . . . ."
How do I communicate about learning using digital evidence?	How to use evidence from observations and conversations to improve my communication with parents about their children's learning	Use evidence from observations and conversations to improve my communication with parents about their children's learning	Using evidence from observations and conversations to improve my communication with parents about their children's learning	Use evidence from observations and conversations to improve their communication with parents about their children's learning

Commitment-Level Application

Working with at least one colleague, explore how you might introduce more pull communication with parents. This will likely involve doing some research into using ePortfolios and available apps that facilitate sharing information with parents about students' learning.

Capacity-Level Application

Find a colleague who's interested in working with you to begin sharing video evidence of students' learning with parents. Review Jackie's explanations of her approach as chapter 5 (page 104) and chapter 6 (page 126) describe. Develop a plan for how you might communicate video evidence of progress to parents.

Confirmation-Level Application

After seeking approval from your principal, set up a study group in your school to explore your reporting formats and procedures. Survey parents about their satisfaction with current methods. Develop a plan for improvement.

Figure 6.18: Shift and Share—Incorporate digital evidence into communication about learning.

Visit go.SolutionTree.com/assessment for a free reproducible version of this figure.

Key Messages

As you reflect on this chapter, we urge you to focus on the following key messages.

1. The traditional push-only method of communicating (focusing on summative data at reporting time) will gradually give way to pull communication (parents, students, and peers have direct and ongoing access to assessment tasks and criteria, feedback, and progress).

2. Communication about learning will become increasingly transparent and open.

3. Technology will make teaching, learning, and assessment increasingly visible to those outside the classroom.

4. Students making mistakes and teachers accepting their flaws will be welcome as essential aspects of learning and growth.

5. Meaningful summaries of learning will increasingly supplement and eventually replace grades.

EPILOGUE

Final Thoughts

We hope that your learning journey through *Rebooting Assessment* has been rich, rewarding, and taken you just a little beyond your comfort level. After all, that is how we all learn! We trust that the numerous video clips throughout this book, serving as exemplars of the VOCAL approach, illustrate the power of technology-supported balanced assessment through conversations and performances in the hands of passionate teachers and their students. Furthermore, we hope we've been successful in convincing you of the vital and empowering role technology (particularly smartphones and tablets) plays in the quest to improve the quality of classroom assessment. We also hope the teacher-readiness scale enables you to develop your skills and understanding within your zone of proximal development (Vygotsky, 1978). Perhaps this is a good time to take one more look at the scale (see figure E.1, page 150). Where do you find yourself now, relative to the descriptors for the four levels?

We certainly understand how daunting it can be when implementing dramatically different practices into your current classroom routines. Please don't feel that you should try to mimic exactly how teachers like Jeff Catania, Jackie Clarke, Holly Moniz, or Jamie Mitchell went about changing their practice (see figure E.2, page 151). They simply provide some examples to support you as you figure out your own approach. Remember that Helen Hills implemented the VOCAL approach to assessment unplugged—that is to say, without using any technology.

Remember, these teachers were also likely in the same place as you at some point in their teaching-with-technology journey. And, of course, their learning doesn't stop. For that reason, all teachers can benefit from a ready, fire, aim approach, especially when taking that first tentative step forward. Notice that in all the Shift and Share figures throughout *Rebooting Assessment*, we urge you to work with one or more colleagues as a collaborative team as you reflect on your current practice and decide what changes to make.

Ultimately, the VOCAL approach is more about relationships than it is about assessment or technology. For everyone involved in education—administrators, teachers,

	Curiosity "I'm curious to learn about . . . ."	Commitment "I'm taking steps and beginning to . . . ."	Capacity "I'm building on my knowledge and skills for . . . ."	Confirmation "I'm proficient at, and helping others to . . . ."
Why should I balance the way I assess student learning?	Why observations of student performance and evidence from conversations might improve the quality and effectiveness of my assessment practice	Explore ways to use observations of student performance and evidence from conversations as part of my assessment practice	Using observations of student performance and evidence from conversations as part of my assessment practice	Use student observations and conversations to improve the quality and effectiveness of their assessment practice
How can digital technology help?	Why technology may or may not have a role in my assessment of student performances and conversations	Collaborate with colleagues who have more expertise to learn to use technology to capture evidence of student performance and conversation	Using technology to capture evidence of student performance and conversation	Use technology to gather, share, and manage evidence of observations and conversations
How do I plan balanced assessment?	Developing assessment plans that include observations and conversations	Develop assessment plans that include evidence from observations and conversations	Developing assessment plans that reflect an appropriate balance of written, oral, and performance evidence	Design assessment plans that include a purposeful balance of written, oral, and performance evidence
How do I assess learning using balanced assessment?	At least one simple way to gather evidence through observations and conversations	Gather evidence of learning through observations and conversations	Gathering evidence through observations and conversations	Gather, share, and involve students in assessing evidence through observations and conversations
How do I use digital technology to implement balanced assessment?	How to watch and assess student performances or interviews live without technology	Allow students to use technology to capture evidence of their learning	Using cloud technology to capture, share, and manage evidence of students' learning	Use technology in a variety of ways to capture evidence of students' learning
How do I support students in curating and sharing their own learning using digital evidence?	How to help students capture evidence from observations and conversations to improve communication with teachers and parents about their learning	Require students to select and review evidence from observations and conversations to improve communication with teachers and parents about their learning	Supporting students in presenting and sharing evidence from observations and conversations to improve communication with teachers and parents about their learning	Enable students to become independent and effective assessors of their own learning and communicating this to others through ePortfolios
How do I use balanced assessment to improve learning?	How to use evidence from observations and conversations with students to help them improve their learning	Use evidence from observations and conversations with students to help them improve their learning	Using evidence from observations and conversations with students to help them improve their learning	Use evidence from observations and conversations with students to help them improve their learning
How do I communicate about learning using digital evidence?	How to use evidence from observations and conversations to improve my communication with parents about their children's learning	Use evidence from observations and conversations to improve my communication with parents about their children's learning	Using evidence from observations and conversations to improve my communication with parents about their children's learning	Use evidence from observations and conversations to improve their communication with parents about their children's learning

Figure E.1: Teacher-readiness scale.

*Visit **go.SolutionTree.com/assessment** for a free reproducible version of this figure.*

and parents—by talking to one another and listening to each unique voice, we develop empathy and understanding so that we all come to value the learning journey together. As Wiggins so wisely reminded educators many years ago, the root of the word *assess* is the Latin word *assidere*, which means *to sit beside* (personal communication, December 1993).

As the case studies and videos illustrate, when mutual respect characterizes the learning environment, good things happen; students engage, discipline issues evaporate, and achievement soars. And so, we invite you to play with observation and conversation in your own classroom (see figure E.3). In so doing, you will strengthen the essential connections between you, your students, and their parents.

Source: © 2017 by Plan Teach Assess. Used with permission.

Figure E.3: The original VOCAL team.

Source: © 2017 by Plan Teach Assess. Used with permission.

Figure E.2: Jeff, Jackie, Holly, Jamie, and Helen use the VOCAL approach.

APPENDIX

Tools to Support
Rebooting Assessment

■ n this appendix, you will find a full list of Shift and Share figures from throughout this book as well as a collection of reproducible resources the teachers featured throughout this book have used in their classrooms. You can also visit **go.SolutionTree.com/assessment** to access them online and print them out for your personal use. We also invite you to access our own personal cloud-based folder of collected tools (visit https://bit.ly/2SRv6Py) on Google Drive, which includes access to original and modified versions of these tools and additional resources we've collected during our VOCAL journey.

List of Video Links

Video 1.1: Diagnostic Interview—https://youtube.com/embed/ptcrL-seJA8?end=40

Video 1.2: Summative Observation—https://youtube.com/embed/uundkIArrzY ?end=40

Video 1.3: Diagnostic Interview—https://youtube.com/embed/rfPX86xd _NA?start=115&end=180

Video 1.4: Group Infomercial Task—https://youtu.be/D0Qz0w8AbyQ

Video 1.5: A Flexible Approach to Summative Assessment—https://youtu.be /Ttte3RJO1Hk

Video 1.6: The Value of the VOCAL Approach—https://youtu.be/iCpzLYX8OF8

Video 2.1: Backward Design in Assessment Planning—https://youtu.be/RD8bInrPL3o

Video 2.2: A Novel Seminar Student Conversation—https://youtu.be/NpS2Giyb1vo

continued →

Video 3.1: Diagnostic Interview and Intervention—https://youtu.be/ptcrL-seJA8

Video 3.2: Collaboration and Student Self-Monitoring—https://youtu.be /KWaSLbvnCoA

Video 3.3: Building a Cooperative Environment—https://youtu.be/0uc9ptXpqEc

Video 3.4: Developing Classroom Community—Part One—https://youtube.com/ embed/kKVwVJycRlw?start=61&end=155

Video 3.5: Developing Classroom Community—Part Two—https://youtube.com/ embed/kKVwVJycRlw?start=182&end=232

Video 3.6: Teacher-Student Reading Conference—https://youtube.com/embed /rfPX86xd_NA?end=52

Video 3.7: Student Reviews Her Performance—https://youtu.be/8a8ywxG3Z4I

Video 3.8: Student Reflects on Her Performance—https://youtu.be/TsftP9eNnnw

Video 3.9: Teacher Gives Instruction for Peer Assessment—https://youtu.be /TnE4FSQ5MxY

Video 3.10: Two Students Engage in Peer Assessment—https://youtu.be /D41WKOIPcrs

Video 4.1: Holly's Technology Journey—https://youtu.be/KpLFRPxm9VY

Video 4.2: Cocreating Assessment Criteria With Students—https://youtube.com /watch?v=GvcomPHZxog&t=86s

Video 4.3: Jackie's Technology Journey—https://youtu.be/3R8FvsJ6XRk

Video 4.4: Unplugged Teacher-Student Interviews—https://youtu.be/Ttte3RJO1Hk

Video 4.5: Unplugged Group Observation (by Teacher)—https://youtu.be /LNzcX6mR04s

Video 4.6: Student-Student Interview—https://youtu.be/D41WKOIPcrs

Video 4.7: Student Group Reflection—https://youtu.be/bh9KSapwIb8

Video 4.8: Interview on the Use of Cloud Tools to Manage Video—https://youtu.be /XdpNcaqB5Lw

Video 5.1: Teacher and Students Cocreated Success Criteria—https://youtu.be /GvcomPHZxog

Video 5.2: A First Cut of a Group Project—https://youtu.be/vQhoXAVrEJA

Video 5.3: Students Discuss Peer Feedback—https://youtu.be/_jo4YOrwHFI

Video 5.4: Students Receive Teacher Feedback—https://youtu.be/0Nr8_7cHJV0

Video 5.5: Teacher Instructions on Using Peer Feedback—https://youtu.be /jumY1frFEmA

Video 5.6: Reading Conference Introduction—https://youtu.be/HuVBb66wr18

Video 5.7: Teacher-Student Reading Interview Conference—https://youtu.be /rfPX86xd_NA

Video 5.8: Teacher-Student Follow-Up Interview—https://youtu.be/TRX3lvzRAI0

Video 5.9: Formative Follow-Up Teacher-Student Interview—https://youtu.be /VtXKvJlkQpc

Video 5.10: Student Peers Use Conversation to Assess for Learning—https://youtu .be/2hN6hu-g-xg

Video 5.11: Teacher Guides Student Peer Coach—https://youtu.be/YS3ZCUl4OPY

Video 5.12: Parent-Student-Teacher Conference—https://youtu.be/-X9bIgFe8gI

Video 6.1: Teacher Interview on Learning, Growth, and the Report Card—https:// youtu .be/v5HSakP58gg

Video 6.2: Three-Way Conference Between Teacher, Student, and Parent—https:// youtu.be/CHjqjvRW-tI

List of *Shift and Share* Figures

continued →

List of Featured Teacher Tools

Sample Parent Letter: Balanced Assessment

Dear Parents or Guardians,

During this school year, our teachers will begin to use a wider variety of assessment types than you have been used to. These will include assessment through observation and assessment through conversation. Why are we making these changes, and what may they look like?

While observing what your children do and listening to what they say were common ways to assess their learning in the early grades, assessment from grades 3 and beyond has tended to rely heavily on written tests, quizzes, and examinations. And while those methods may have served us reasonably well when teaching and learning were concerned primarily with acquiring lots of knowledge, our world today is changing rapidly.

Your children are expected to develop increasingly complex skills and competencies in order to be successful once they graduate. And so in addition to literacy and numeracy, children are developing the skills of critical thinking and problem solving, creativity and innovation, communication and collaboration, flexibility and adaptability, initiative and self-direction, social and cross-cultural skills, leadership and responsibility, life and career skills, as well as information, media, and technology skills.

Yes, it's quite a daunting list! And we are sure you can see how we can no longer rely primarily on traditional testing to assess your children's learning and inform you about their successes and areas of need.

That is why our teachers will be making increasing use of observation and conversation to assess your children's learning, with much of it occurring while the learning is occurring—what is called *formative assessment*.

With your written permission, some teachers will be using the recording functions on smartphones, tablets, and other devices to capture digital evidence of your child's learning. Over time, you can expect your child and his or her teachers to begin sharing brief recordings with you, both to keep you informed about your child's progress, and so you may support further learning at home.

As always, we welcome your questions and inquiries if you wish to learn more about this move to more balanced assessment.

Yours sincerely,

Reading Conference Template: Primary Language

Reading Conference

Parent and Child

Name:	Date of Conference:

Conference Steps:

☐ Access our online class page.

☐ Watch video recording of reading.

☐ Review reading response—have your child explain his or her strengths and next steps.

Prompting questions:

- Why do you feel _____ is one of your reading strengths?
- How does _____ strategy help you as a reader?
- Why do you think _____ is a good next step for you as a reader?
- How will _____ help you to improve your reading?

☐ Provide your child with feedback—What did he or she do *really well* as a reader? How will you *support* him or her in the next steps at home? What reading goals did he or she develop with me?

☐ Celebrate his or her reading success!

Source: © 2016 by Jackie Clarke. Adapted with permission.

Reading Response Observation: Primary Language

Reading Response—Observational Notes

Name:	Book Title:

Before Reading:

- Book summary: _____
- Prereading questions: _____
- Read _____ and record your response in the next section.

During Reading:

After Reading:

- List a *STAR* and a WISH.

- What reading strategy did you use?

- Question 1: _____?

- Question 2: _____?

- Question 3: _____?

Source: © 2016 by Jackie Clarke. Adapted with permission.

Student Goal Bookmarks: Primary Language

REMAIN CALM AND READ ON

_____'s
reading goals!

My goals are . . .

_____

_____

_____

_____

_____

_____

_____

_____

REMAIN CALM AND READ ON

_____'s
reading goals!

My goals are . . .

_____

_____

_____

_____

_____

_____

_____

_____

REMAIN CALM AND READ ON

_____'s
reading goals!

My goals are . . .

_____

_____

_____

_____

_____

_____

_____

_____

Source: © 2016 by Jackie Clarke. Adapted with permission.

Teacher Planning Template

Guiding Questions	Example Look-Fors	Purpose
Planning for Learning • How do you use the backward-design model to plan for student learning? • How do you plan your assessment methods to ensure a balanced approach to observation, conversation, and product evidence? • How do you purposefully plan assessment methods that incorporate technology? • How do you set up your classroom (program and routines) to allow for collection of digital evidence? *For example, if the teacher collects data one-to-one, how do you ensure an environment that allows for collecting this type of evidence?*	• Long-range planning tools • Classroom cocreated expectations and norms • Classroom tour to show learning environment	• Model for educators how to use the backward-design planning model. • Model for educators how to plan for assessment to ensure a balanced approach. • Model for educators how to integrate technology into the assessment process and purposefully plan for its implementation. • Model for educators how to structure classroom routines and expectations to allow for collection of digital evidence.
Gathering Digital Evidence • What types of digital evidence (conversations or performances) do you choose to record? *For example, reading conferences, mathematics congresses, peer feedback on a drama presentation, and so on* • What is the purpose of recording this evidence? • What method of technology (*iPad, smartphone, Chromebook*) do you use to collect evidence of conversations and performances? • Who is doing the recording? • Where is the digital evidence stored?	• Recording forms to direct conferences • Conferencing and feedback • Video footage of collected digital evidence	• Model for educators what types of technology to use to collect digital evidence. • Model for educators the types of assessment data they can capture digitally. • Model for educators how to capture digital evidence in a classroom setting.
Using Digital Evidence in the Classroom • How do you use these digital recordings for assessment purposes? How do they impact your teaching practice? How do they impact student learning? • Do students interact with the recordings, or are they for teacher use only? If students do access the digital recordings, what is the purpose? *For example, students conference with a teacher or peer, complete a reflection, and so on.* • How do you justify your conversation- and performance-based recordings to students, parents, and administrators? • Do you grade your digital recordings? How do you use these recordings as demonstrations of learning?	• Recording forms to direct conferences • Notes and information shared with families, administrators, or both to justify digital evidence • Shared rubrics, checklists, and grade books (paper or digital) to show how you record digital footage as evidence of learning	• Model for educators how you use this type of assessment to make purposeful and data-driven instructions for student learning. • Model for educators how to involve students in the assessment cycle and interact with their own learning and goal setting. • Model for educators how to effectively share digital recordings with students, families, and the school community.

Source: © 2016 by Jackie Clarke. Used with permission.

Group Performance Success Criteria Checklist and Feedback

Please use this cocreated checklist to provide positive, constructive feedback for the group videos that you are assessing during our peer feedback–loop cycle. Keep one chart per group, and add multiple comments in the boxes provided. If you could use a different color for your feedback than the previous group, that would be awesome! Thanks!

Criteria (Outlined expectations)	**Descriptive Feedback** (Provide comments.)	**En Route** (Check off with X.)	**Met**	**Exceeded**
Oral communication: Clear and loud voice, eye contact, comfort with the lines, appropriate projection, pace, and speed to ensure audience understanding and engagement				
Media literacy: Use of media component as a prop, physical props, testimonials as a feature of infomercials, animations within supports, knowing your target audience				
Drama: Engaging host character, staying in role, purposely being over the top				
Reading: Understanding of the text, able to hook the audience with the big ideas without spoiling the book ending, use of direct quotes and evidence				
Next steps:				

Source: © 2016 by Holly Moniz. Used with permission.

Interview Look-Fors and Teacher Prompts: Senior Mathematics

Performance Task Interview

Student Name: _____

Task	Incorrect, major error	With assistance	Independently	Level	Description (List the success criteria for each proficiency level.)
				4	
				3	
				2	

Look-Fors

Notes:

Teacher Talk Prompts

- "How did you know that wasn't the one?"
- "Please show me how you did that."
- "Help me understand what you're thinking here."
- "Can you explain how you got . . . ?"
- "Are you saying . . . ?" "What does _____ mean?"
- "What else can you add to your answer?"
- "I'm unclear about how you . . . "
- "How is this different from . . . ?"
- "Can you do this another way?"
- "How could you check your calculations?"

Source: © 2016 by Stephanie Girvan. Adapted with permission.

References and Resources

Allal, L. (2013). Teachers' professional judgement in assessment: A cognitive act and a socially situated practice. *Assessment in Education: Principles, Policy and Practice, 20*(1), 20–34.

Bailey, K., & Jakicic, C. (2017). *Simplifying common assessment: A guide for Professional Learning Communities at Work.* Bloomington, IN: Solution Tree Press.

Bandura, A. (1989). Regulation of cognitive processes through perceived self-efficacy. *Developmental Psychology, 25*(5), 729–735.

Bandura, A. (1994). Self-efficacy. In V. S. Ramachaudran (Ed.), *Encyclopedia of human behavior* (Vol. 4, pp. 71–81). New York: Academic Press. (Reprinted in H. Friedman [Ed.], Encyclopedia of mental health. San Diego: Academic Press, 1998).

Bedell, C. (2014). *The state of cloud computing in K–12.* Accessed at https://webobjects .cdw.com/webobjects/media/pdf/Solutions/Cloud-Computing/111414-K-12TechDeci sions-TheStateofCloudComputing-K-12.pdf on May 4, 2021.

Bjork, E. L., & Bjork, R. A. (2014). Making things hard on yourself, but in a good way: Creating desirable difficulties to enhance learning. In M. A. Gernsbacher & J. R. Pomerantz (Eds.), *Psychology and the real world: Essays illustrating fundamental contributions to society* (2nd ed., pp. 59–68). New York: Worth.

Black, P., Harrison, C., Lee, C., Marshall, B., & Wiliam, D. (2003). *Assessment for learning: Putting it into practice.* Berkshire, England: Open University Press.

Black, P., Harrison, C., Lee, C., Marshall, B., & Wiliam, D. (2004). Working inside the black box: Assessment for learning in the classroom. *Phi Delta Kappan, 86*(1), 8–21. Accessed at www.researchgate.net/publication/44835745_Working_Inside_the _Black_Box_Assessment_for_Learning_in_the_Classroom on October 20, 2020.

Black, P., & Wiliam, D. (1998). Inside the black box: Raising standards through classroom assessment. *Phi Delta Kappan, 80*(2), 144, 146–148. Accessed at https:// kappanonline.org/inside-the-black-box-raising-standards-through-classroom -assessment on October 20, 2020.

Black, P., & Wiliam, D. (2004). The formative purpose: Assessment must first promote learning. *Yearbook of the National Society for the Study of Education, 103*(2), 20–50.

Blackburn, B. R. (2018). Productive struggle is a learner's sweet spot. *Productive Struggle for All, 14*(11). Accessed at www.ascd.org/ascd-express/vol14/num11/productive-struggle-is-a-learners-sweet-spot.aspx on February 3, 2021.

Boudett, K. P., City, E. A., & Murnane, R. J. (Eds.). (2013). *Data wise: A step-by-step guide to using assessment results to improve teaching and learning* (Rev. and expanded ed.). Cambridge, MA: Harvard Education Press.

British Columbia's (BC's) Curriculum. (n.d.). *Critical thinking & reflective thinking.* Accessed at https://curriculum.gov.bc.ca/competencies/thinking/critical-and-reflective-thinking on May 7, 2021.

Broadfoot, P., Daugherty, R., Gardner, J., & Gipps, C. (1999, June). *Assessment for learning: Beyond the black box.* Cambridge, England: University of Cambridge School of Education.

Castelo, M. (2020, July 1). The IT investment priorities shaping today's school districts. *EdTech: Focus on K–12.* Accessed at https://edtechmagazine.com/k12/article/2020/07/it-investment-priorities-shaping-todays-school-districts on October 19, 2020.

Catania, J., Dalrymple, S., & Gadanidis, G. (2003). *The joy of x: Mathematics teaching in grades 7–12.* Published by MathMania.

Chappuis, J., & Stiggins, R. (2020). *Classroom assessment* for *student learning: Doing it right—Using it well* (3rd ed.). Boston: Pearson Education.

Chen, J. (2021, January 27). Group of seven (G-7). *Investopedia.* Accessed at www.investopedia.com/terms/g/g7.asp on April 13, 2021.

Cody, A., & Bower, J. (2013, March 13). *Bill Gates and the cult of measurement: Efficiency without excellence* [Blog post]. Accessed at https://nepc.colorado.edu/blog/bill-gates-and-cult-measurement-efficiency-without-excellence on June 2, 2021.

Cohen, M. (1996). *Lost in the museum.* New York: Yearling Books.

Cohen, R. K., Opatosky, D. K., Savage, J., Stevens, S. O., & Darrah, E. P. (2021). *The metacognitive student: How to teach academic, social, and emotional intelligence in every content area.* Bloomington, IN: Solution Tree Press.

Cooper, D. (2007). *Talk about assessment: Strategies and tools to improve learning.* Scarborough, Ontario, Canada: Nelson Education.

Cooper, D. (2010). *Talk about assessment: High school strategies and tools.* Scarborough, Ontario, Canada: Nelson Education.

Cooper, D. (2011). *Redefining fair: How to plan, assess, and grade for excellence in mixed-ability classrooms.* Bloomington, IN: Solution Tree Press.

Cooper, D. (2016). *A solution to the surprise report card* [Blog post]. Accessed at https://freshgrade.com/blog/a-solution-to-the-surprise-report-card on November 5, 2020.

Cooper, D. (2017). *What is "triangulation" in the assessment context?* [Blog post]. Accessed at https://freshgrade.com/blog/what-is-triangulation-in-the-assessment-context on January 25, 2021.

Cortez, M. B. (2017, September 5). Cloud computer for K–12 will see steady growth through 2021. *EdTech: Focus on K–12.* Accessed at https://edtechmagazine.com/k12 /article/2017/09/cloud-computing-k-12-will-see-steady-growth-through-2021 on May 4, 2021.

Crockett, L. W., & Churches, A. (2018). *Growing global digital citizens: Better practices that build better learners.* Bloomington, IN: Solution Tree Press.

Darling-Hammond, L., & McCloskey, L. (2008). Assessment for learning around the world: What would it mean to be internationally competitive? *Phi Delta Kappan, 90*(4), 263–272.

Davies, A. (2011). *Making classroom assessment work* (3rd ed.). Bloomington, IN: Solution Tree Press.

Denzin, N. K. (Ed.). (2017). *The research act: A theoretical introduction to sociological methods.* New York: Routledge. (Original work published 1970)

DuFour, R., DuFour, R., Eaker, R., Many, T. W., & Mattos, M. (2016). *Learning by doing: A handbook for Professional Learning Communities at Work* (3rd ed.). Bloomington, IN: Solution Tree Press.

Dweck, C. S. (2006). Mindset: *The new psychology of success.* New York: Ballantine Books.

Dweck, C. S. (2016). *Mindset: The new psychology of success* (Updated ed.). New York: Ballantine Books.

Earl, L. M. (2004). *Assessment as learning: Using classroom assessment to maximize student learning.* Thousand Oaks, CA: Corwin Press.

Earl, L. M. (2007). Assessment as learning. In W. D. Hawley (Ed.), *The keys to effective schools: Educational reform as continuous improvement* (pp. 85–97). Thousand Oaks, CA: Corwin Press.

Earl, L. M. (2013). *Assessment as learning: Using classroom assessment to maximize student learning* (2nd ed.). Thousand Oaks, CA: Corwin Press.

Ellington, B. J. (1981). The Cloze procedure. *Journal of Research and Development, 14*(4), 94–96.

Eyal, L. (2012). Digital assessment literacy: The core role of the teacher in a digital environment. *Educational Technology and Society, 15*(2), 37–49.

Fisher, D., & Frey, N. (2014). *Better learning through structured teaching: A framework for the gradual release of responsibility* (2nd ed.). Alexandria, VA: Association for Supervision and Curriculum Development.

Fullan, M. (2011). *Motion leadership: The skinny on becoming change savvy.* Thousand Oaks, CA: Corwin Press. Accessed at https://michaelfullan.ca/wp-content/uploads /2016/06/11_TheSkinny_US.compressed.pdf on April 22, 2021.

Grafwallner, P. (2021). *Not yet . . . and that's OK: How productive struggle fosters student learning.* Bloomington, IN: Solution Tree Press.

Guskey, T. R. (2011). Five obstacles to grading reform. *Educational Leadership, 69*(3), 16–21. Accessed at www.ascd.org/publications/educational-leadership/nov11/vol69 /num03/Five-Obstacles-to-Grading-Reform.aspx on May 10, 2021.

Guskey, T. R. (2013). The case against percentage grades. *Educational Leadership, 71*(1), 68–72. Accessed at https://tguskey.com/wp-content/uploads/Grading-2-The-Case -Against-Percentage-Grades.pdf on April 26, 2021.

Guskey, T. R. (2015). *On your mark: Challenging the conventions of grading and reporting.* Bloomington, IN: Solution Tree Press.

Hamilton, E. R., Rosenberg, J. M., & Akcaoglu, M. (2016). The substitution of augmentation modification redefinition (SAMR) model: A critical review and suggestions for its use. *TechTrends, 60,* 443–441.

Hansen, J. (2020, November 30). *COVID-19 pushes schools to their limit, and the cloud shows its worth.* Accessed at https://orangematter.solarwinds.com/2020/11/30/covid -19-pushes-schools-to-their-limit-and-the-cloud-shows-its-worth on May 4, 2021.

Hattie, J. (2009). *Visible learning: A synthesis of over 800 meta-analyses relating to achievement.* New York: Routledge.

Hattie, J. (2012). *Visible learning for teachers: Maximizing impact on learning.* New York: Routledge.

Hattie, J., & Clarke, S. (2019). *Visible learning: Feedback.* New York: Routledge.

Hattie, J., & Timperley, H. (2007). The power of feedback. *Review of Educational Research, 77*(1), 81–112.

Hill, P., & Barber, M. (2014, December). *Preparing for a renaissance in assessment.* London: Pearson. Accessed at www.pearson.com/content/dam/one-dot-com/one -dot-com/uk/documents/educator/primary/preparing_for_a_renaissance_in _assessment_and_summary_text_december_2014.pdf on April 6, 2021.

Irani, A. (2007). *The song of Kahunsha.* Minneapolis, MN: Milkweed Editions.

James, M. (2017). Embedding formative assessment in classroom practice. In R. Maclean (Ed.), *Life in schools and classrooms: Past, present and future* (pp. 509–525). Singapore: Spring Nature. Accessed at www.researchgate.net/publication/316733898 _Embedding_Formative_Assessment_in_Classroom_Practice on June 30, 2021.

Joint Information Systems Committee. (2020, Spring). *The future of assessment: Five principles, five targets for 2025.* Accessed at https://repository.jisc.ac.uk/7733/1 /the-future-of-assessment-report.pdf on April 26, 2021.

Kerr, D., Heller, J., Hulen, T. A., & Butler, B. K. (2021). *What about us? The PLC at Work process for grades preK–2 teams.* Bloomington, IN: Solution Tree Press.

Kise, J. A. G. (2021). *Doable differentiation: Twelve strategies to meet the needs of all learners.* Bloomington, IN: Solution Tree Press.

Knight, S., & Smith, R. (2010, June). *Effective assessment in a digital age: A guide to technology-enhanced assessment and feedback.* PowerPoint presented at the Higher Education Academy Annual Conference, Hertfordshire, England. Accessed at www.advance-he.ac.uk/knowledge-hub/effective-assessment-digital-age -guide-technology-enhanced-assessment-and-feedback on May 24, 2021.

Kolk, M. (n.d.). Embrace action research: Improve classroom practice with action research . . . and tell the story. *Creative Educator.* Accessed at https:// thecreativeeducator.com/v07/articles/Embracing_Action_Research on May 10, 2021.

Kutanis, R. Ö., & Mesci, M. (2011). The effects of locus of control on learning performance: A case of an academic organization. *Journal of Economic and Social Studies, 1*(2), 113–136.

Lartaud, D. (2015, November 16). *Science spotlight: How your smartphone knows where you are.* Accessed at www.kqed.org/quest/97280/how-your-smartphone-knows -where-you-are on April 28, 2021.

McTighe, J., & Curtis, G. (2019). *Leading modern learning: A blueprint for vision-driven schools* (2nd ed.). Bloomington, IN: Solution Tree Press.

McTighe, J., Doubet, K. J., & Carbaugh, E. M. (2020). *Designing authentic performance tasks and projects: Tools for meaningful learning and assessment.* Alexandria, VA: Association for Supervision and Curriculum Development.

Moss, C. M., & Brookhart, S. M. (2019). *Advancing formative assessment in every classroom: A guide for instructional leaders* (2nd ed.). Alexandria, VA: Association for Supervision and Curriculum Development.

Niemi, K. (2020, December 15). *Niemi: CASEL is updating the most widely recognized definition of social-emotional learning—Here's why* [Letter to the editor]. Accessed at www.the74million.org/article/niemi-casel-is-updating-the-most-widely-recognized -definition-of-social-emotional-learning-heres-why on May 3, 2021.

Nowicki, S., & Strickland, B. R. (1973). A locus of control scale for children. *Journal of Consulting and Clinical Psychology, 40*(1), 148–154.

O'Connor, K. (2011). *A repair kit for grading: 15 fixes for broken grades.* Boston: Pearson Education.

O'Connor, K. (2018). *How to grade for learning: Linking grades to sstandards* (4th ed.). Thousand Oaks, CA: Corwin Press.

Oldfield, A., Broadfoot, R., Timmis, S., & Timmis, S. (n.d.). *Assessment in a digital age: A research review.* Accessed at www.bristol.ac.uk/media-library/sites/education /documents/researchreview.pdf on September 29, 2020.

Ontario Ministry of Education. (2007a). *The Ontario curriculum grades 1–8: Science and technology.* Accessed at www.edu.gov.on.ca/eng/curriculum/elementary /scientec18currb.pdf on July 20, 2021.

Ontario Ministry of Education. (2007b). *The Ontario curriculum grades 9 and 10: English.* Accessed at www.edu.gov.on.ca/eng/curriculum/secondary/ english910currb.pdf on April 14, 2021.

Ontario Ministry of Education. (2010). *Growing success: Assessment, evaluation, and reporting in Ontario schools.* Accessed at www.edu.gov.on.ca/eng/policyfunding /growSuccess.pdf on September 14, 2020.

Onuscheck, M., & Spiller, J. (Eds.). (2020). *Reading and writing instruction for fourth- and fifth-grade classrooms in a PLC at Work.* Bloomington, IN: Solution Tree Press.

Palao, J. M., Hastie, P. A., Cruz, P. G., & Ortega, E. (2015). The impact of video technology on student performance in physical education. *Technology, Pedagogy and Education, 24*(1), 51–63.

Partnership for 21st Century Learning. (2019). *Framework for 21st century learning.* Accessed at http://static.battelleforkids.org/documents/p21/P21_Framework_Brief .pdf on April 27, 2021.

Pearson, P. D., & Gallagher, M. C. (1983, October). *The instruction of reading comprehension* (Technical Report No. 297). Champaign: University of Illinois at Urbana-Champaign, Center for the Study of Reading.

Phelan, C., & Wren, J. (2005–2006). *Exploring reliability in academic assessment.* Accessed at https://chfasoa.uni.edu/reliabilityandvalidity.htm on May 24, 2021.

Race, P., Brown, S., & Smith, B. (2005). *500 tips on assessment* (2nd ed.). New York: Routledge.

Rebooting Assessment. (2021a, July 30). *Classroom voices on the value of conversation and observation* [Video file]. Accessed at https://youtu.be/iCpzLYX8OF8 on August 1, 2021.

Rebooting Assessment. (2021b, July 30). *Diagnostic interview and intervention (grade 9 mathematics)* [Video file]. Accessed at https://youtu.be/ptcrL-seJA8 on August 1, 2021.

Rebooting Assessment. (2021c, July 30). *Explicit teaching of feedback process* [Video file]. Accessed at https://youtu.be/jumY1frFEmA on August 1, 2021.

Rebooting Assessment. (2021d, July 30). *Follow up reading interview* [Video file]. Accessed at https://youtu.be/TRX3lvzRAI0 on August 1, 2021.

Rebooting Assessment. (2021e, July 30). *Formative follow-up interview with unfamiliar passage* [Video file]. Accessed at https://youtu.be/VtXKvJlkQpc on August 1, 2021.

Rebooting Assessment. (2021f, July 30). *Formative student-student interview (grade 9 mathematics)* [Video file]. Accessed at https://youtu.be/D41WKOIPcrs on August 1, 2021.

Rebooting Assessment. (2021g, July 30). *Holly's technology journey* [Video file]. Accessed at https://youtu.be/KpLFRPxm9VY on August 1, 2021.

Rebooting Assessment. (2021h, July 30). *Jackie's technology journey* [Video file]. Accessed at https://youtu.be/3R8FvsJ6XRk on August 1, 2021.

Rebooting Assessment. (2021i, July 30). *Novel seminar conversation (final evaluation, grade 9 English)* [Video file]. Accessed at https://youtu.be/NpS2Giyb1vo on August 1, 2021.

Rebooting Assessment. (2021j, July 30). *Novel seminar observation (final evaluation, grade 9 English)* [Video file]. Accessed at https://youtu.be/uundkIArrzY on August 1, 2021.

Rebooting Assessment. (2021k, July 30). *Peer conversation feedback* [Video file]. Accessed at https://youtu.be/2hN6hu-g-xg on August 1, 2021.

Rebooting Assessment. (2021l, July 30). *Peer conversation feedback with teacher* [Video file]. Accessed at https://youtu.be/YS3ZCUl4OPY on August 1, 2021.

Rebooting Assessment. (2021m, July 30). *Reading conference introduction* [Video file]. Accessed at https://youtu.be/HuVBb66wr18 on August 1, 2021.

Rebooting Assessment. (2021n, August 1). *Student feedback during performance* [Video file]. Accessed at https://youtu.be/vQhoXAVrEJA on August 1, 2021.

Rebooting Assessment. (2021o, July 30). *Student reviewing their own performance: Self-reflection* [Video file]. Accessed at https://youtu.be/8a8ywxG3Z4I on August 1, 2021.

Rebooting Assessment. (2021p, July 30). *Student self-reflecting after watching her own performance* [Video file]. Accessed at https://youtu.be/TsftP9eNnnw on August 1, 2021.

Rebooting Assessment. (2021q, July 30). *Student-parent-teacher conference introduction* [Video file]. Accessed at https://youtu.be/-X9bIgFe8gI on August 1, 2021.

Rebooting Assessment. (2021r, July 30). *Student-teacher co-created assessment criteria (checkbric)* [Video file]. Accessed at https://youtu.be/GvcomPHZxog on August 1, 2021.

Rebooting Assessment. (2021s, July 30). *Student-teacher reading interview conference (primary language)* [Video file]. Accessed at https://youtu.be/rfPX86xd_NA on August 1, 2021.

Rebooting Assessment. (2021t, July 30). *Student-teacher summative interview (grade 10 mathematics)* [Video file]. Accessed at https://youtu.be/Ttte3RJO1Hk on August 1, 2021.

Rebooting Assessment. (2021u, July 30). *Students reviewing own performance with peer feedback (intermediate language)* [Video file]. Accessed at https://youtu.be/_jo4YOrwHFI on August 1, 2021.

Rebooting Assessment. (2021v, August 1). *Students reviewing their own performance* [Video file]. Accessed at https://youtu.be/vQhoXAVrEJA on August 1, 2021.

Rebooting Assessment. (2021w, July 30). *Summative group conversation with teacher observation* [Video file]. Accessed at https://youtu.be/LNzcX6mR04s on August 1, 2021.

Rebooting Assessment. (2021x, July 30). *Teacher conference with student and parent* [Video file]. Accessed at https://youtu.be/CHjqjvRW-tI on August 1, 2021.

Rebooting Assessment. (2021y, July 30). *Teacher instructions for student recorded feedback on summative question and response* [Video file]. Accessed at https://youtu.be/TnE4FSQ5MxY on August 1, 2021.

Rebooting Assessment. (2021z, July 30). *Teacher interview: Backward design in assessment planning* [Video file]. Accessed at https://youtu.be/RD8bInrPL3o on August 1, 2021.

Rebooting Assessment. (2021aa, July 30). *Teacher interview: Building a cooperative environment* [Video file]. Accessed at https://youtu.be/0uc9ptXpqEc on August 1, 2021.

Rebooting Assessment. (2021bb, July 30). *Teacher interview: Developing classroom community* [Video file]. Accessed at https://youtu.be/kKVwVJycRlw on August 1, 2021.

Rebooting Assessment. (2021cc, July 30). *Teacher interview: On collaboration and student self-monitoring* [Video file]. Accessed at https://youtu.be/KWaSLbvnCoA on August 1, 2021.

Rebooting Assessment. (2021dd, July 30). *Teacher interview on learning, growth and the report card* [Video file]. Accessed at https://youtu.be/v5HSakP58gg on August 1, 2021.

Rebooting Assessment. (2021ee, July 30). *Teacher interview on use of cloud tools to manage video* [Video file]. Accessed at https://youtu.be/XdpNcaqB5Lw on August 1, 2021.

Rebooting Assessment. (2021ff, July 30). *Teacher oral formative feedback* [Video file]. Accessed at https://youtu.be/0Nr8_7cHJV0 on August 1, 2021.

Rebooting Assessment. (2021gg, July 30). *Teacher recording group presentations (intermediate language)* [Video file]. Accessed at https://youtu.be/D0Qz0w8AbyQ on August 1, 2021.

Reeves, D. (2016). *Elements of grading: A guide to effective practice* (2nd ed.). Bloomington, IN: Solution Tree Press.

Reid, D. A., Simmt, E., Savard, A., Suurtamm, C., Manuel, D., Lin, T. W. J., et al. (2015). Observing observers: Using video to prompt and record reflections on teachers' pedagogies in four regions of Canada. *Research in Comparative & International Education, 10*(3), 367–382.

RM Results. (n.d.). *Qualifying the skills of the future: Education and assessment reform around the world* [White paper]. Oxfordshire, England: RM Education.

Romrell, D., Kidder, L., & Wood, E. (2014). The SAMR model as a framework for evaluating mlearning. *Online Learning Journal, 18*(2).

Ronen, M., & Langley, D. (2004). Scaffolding complex tasks by open online submission: Emerging patterns and profiles. *Journal of Asynchronous Learning Networks, 8*(4), 39–61.

Schacter, J. (2000). Does individual tutoring produce optimal learning? *American Educational Research Journal, 37*(3), 801–829.

Schiller, D., Freeman, J. B., Mitchell, J. P., Uleman, J. S., & Phelps, E. A. (2009). A neural mechanism of first impressions. *Nature Neuroscience, 12*(4), 508–514.

Stiggins, R. J. (1994). *Student-centered classroom assessment.* New York: Macmillan.

Stiggins, R. J. (2005, September). *Assessment* for *learning defined.* Presented at ETS/Assessment Training Institute's International Conference, Promoting Sound Assessment in Every Classroom, Portland, OR.

Stiggins, R. (2009). Assessment *for* learning in upper elementary grades. *Phi Delta Kappan, 90*(6), 419–421.

Stiggins, R. (2020, May 6). *Support all students, especially the most vulnerable* [Blog post]. Accessed at https://rickstiggins.com/2020/05/06/support-all-student-especially-the-most-vulnerable on April 29, 2020.

Stiggins, R. J., Arter, J. A., Chappuis, J., & Chappuis, S. (2004). *Classroom assessment for student learning: Doing it right—using it well.* Portland, OR: Assessment Training Institute.

Sutton, R. (1991). *Assessment: A framework for teachers.* Windsor, Berkshire, England: NFER-Nelson.

Tailab, M., & Marsh, N. (2019). Use of self-assessment of video recording to raise students' awareness of development of their oral presentation skills. *Higher Education Studies, 10*(1), 16–28.

Townsley, M., & Wear, N. L. (2020). *Making grades matter: Standards-based grading in a secondary PLC at Work.* Bloomington, IN: Solution Tree Press.

Van der Kleij, F., Adie, L., & Cumming, J. (2017). Using video technology to enable student voice in assessment feedback. *British Journal of Educational Technology, 48*(5), 1092–1105.

Vasylyna, N. (2011, February 25). *Pareto Principle in software testing* [Blog post]. Accessed at https://blog.qatestlab.com/2011/02/25/pareto-principle-in-software-testing on May 5, 2021.

Vygotsky, L. S. (1978). *Mind in society. The development of higher psychological processes.* Cambridge, MA: Harvard University Press.

Watson, A. (n.d.). *Classroom management in the BYOD classroom.* Accessed at https://thecornerstoneforteachers.com/classroom-management-in-the-byod-classroom on January 23, 2021.

Wiggins, G. (1998). *Educative assessment: Designing assessments to inform and improve student performance.* San Francisco: Jossey-Bass.

Wiggins, G., & McTighe, J. (2005). *Understanding by design* (Expanded 2nd ed.). Alexandria, VA: Association for Supervision and Curriculum Development.

Wilczek, F. (2015, September 23). Einstein's parable of quantum insanity. *Scientific American*. Accessed at www.scientificamerican.com/article/einstein-s-parable-of -quantum-insanity on April 6, 2021.

Wiliam, D. (2011). *Embedded formative assessment.* Bloomington, IN: Solution Tree Press.

Wiliam, D. (2018). *Embedded formative assessment* (2nd ed.). Bloomington, IN: Solution Tree Press.

Wormeli, R. (2006). *Fair isn't always equal: Assessing and grading in the differentiated classroom.* Portland, ME: Stenhouse.

Wormeli, R. (2018). *Fair isn't always equal: Assessment and grading in the differentiated classroom* (2nd ed.). Portland, ME: Stenhouse.

Zetlin, M. (2016, July 31). *Here's how to keep a tech failure from derailing your presentation* [Blog post]. Accessed at www.inc.com/minda-zetlin/heres-how-to-keep-a-tech -failure-from-derailing-your-presentation.html on May 5, 2021.

Zimmer, D., Kirkpatrick, C., Montesanto, R., Suurtamm, C., Trew, S., & Charbonneau, D. (2001). *Mathematics 10.* Scarborough, Ontario, Canada: Nelson Thomson Learning. Accessed at https://melochesmath.weebly.com/ uploads/2/3/2/1/23212488 /pg_1-44.pdf on May 24, 2021.

Index

Redefining Fair
Damian Cooper

Learn how to define proficiency accurately and differentiate to help all students achieve it. Using stories, strategies, case histories, and sample documents, the author explains how to implement equitable instruction, assessment, grading, and reporting practices for diverse 21st century learners.
BKF412

Shifting to Digital
James A. Bellanca, Gwendolyn Battle Lavert, and Kate Bellanca

Rely on *Shifting to Digital* to give you clear, concise, and helpful answers to all of your remote teaching questions. This comprehensive guide provides specific strategies for planning high-engagement instruction, handling technology, assessing collaboration and assignments, and more.
BKG006

Personalized Deeper Learning
James A. Bellanca

Foster deeper learning with two templates—one for students, the other for teachers—that increase student agency and learning transfer within critical skill sets. Any teacher—regardless of grade, existing curriculum, or student load—can adapt, scale, and sustain these powerful personalized learning plans.
BKF975

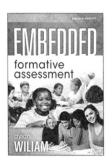

Embedded Formative Assessment (Second Edition)
Dylan Wiliam

The second edition of this best-selling resource presents new research, insights, examples, and formative assessment techniques teachers can immediately apply in their classrooms. Updated examples and templates help teachers elicit evidence of learning, provide meaningful feedback, and empower students to take ownership of their education.
BKF790

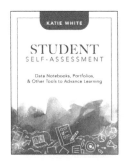

Student Self-Assessment
Katie White

Increase the achievement of every learner with *Student Self-Assessment*. In this practical guide, author Katie White outlines how to plan and implement various self-assessment strategies to ensure student growth at all grade levels. She covers every stage of the process—from setup to goal setting to celebrating.
BKG038

Solution Tree | Press

a division of
Solution Tree

Visit SolutionTree.com or call 800.733.6786 to order.

Excellent engagement
in what truly matters
in **assessment.**

Great examples!

PD Services

Our experts draw from decades of research and their own experiences to bring you practical strategies for designing and implementing quality assessments. You can choose from a range of customizable services, from a one-day overview to a multiyear process.

Book your assessment PD today!
888.763.9045

Solution Tree